S0-DQX-453

THE PICTURE ATLAS
OF THE WORLD

Illustrated by Brian Delf

M&S

A DORLING KINDERSLEY BOOK

Text by Richard Kemp

Art Editor Lester Cheeseman
Designer Marcus James
Project Editor Susan Peach
Senior Editor Emma Johnson
Consultant Keith Lye
Production Teresa Solomon
Art Director Roger Priddy

First published in Great Britain in 1991
by Dorling Kindersley Limited,
9 Henrietta Street, London WC2E 8PS

First published in Canada in 1991 by
McClelland & Stewart Inc.
The Canadian Publishers
481 University Avenue
Toronto, Ontario
M5G 2E9

Canadian Cataloguing in Publication Data

Delf, Brian.
    The picture atlas of the world

ISBN 0-7710-7030-6

1. Atlases – Juvenile literature. I. Kemp,
Richard.

G1021.D43 1991   j912   C91-093457-6

Reproduced in Hong Kong by Bright Arts
Printed and bound in Italy by New Interlitho, Milan

CONTENTS

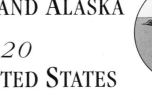

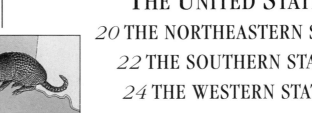

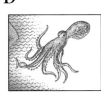

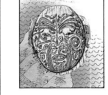

OUR PLANET EARTH

THE EARTH on which we live is one of a family of nine planets which circle around a star called the sun. The sun is just one of about 100 billion stars in our galaxy. On a clear night you can see some of the other stars in the galaxy as a glow in the sky, called the milky way. Astronomers estimate that there may be as many as 10 billion galaxies, which together make up the universe.

THE SOLAR SYSTEM

The sun is much bigger than the planets. It has a diameter of about 864,948 miles (1,392,000 km). The diameter of the earth at the equator is only 7,747 miles (12,714 km).

The distance from the sun to the earth is about 93 million miles (150 million km). If a train left earth at a speed of 110 mph (175 kph), it would take 96 years to reach the sun.

THE ATMOSPHERE

The atmosphere is a layer of gases surrounding the earth. It is about 621 miles (1,000 km) thick and is made of nitrogen, oxygen, carbon dioxide, water vapor, and small amounts of other gases. The atmosphere acts as a protective shield, absorbing much of the heat that reaches the earth from the sun. Without it, our whole planet would be burnt to a desert.

Most of the gases in the atmosphere are concentrated in the lowest part, which is called the troposphere. Above this is the stratosphere. This contains the ozone layer, which absorbs harmful ultraviolet rays from the sun. Above the stratosphere are the mesosphere and the thermosphere. Here the gases are so thin that there is little difference between these parts of the atmosphere and space.

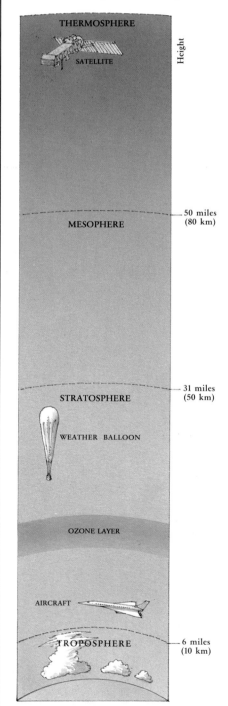

THE EARTH'S SHIELD

The earth is like a giant magnet. It has two magnetic poles, which lie near the north and south poles. The earth's magnetism is probably caused by movement of the molten metals in its outer core. Around the earth is a region called the magnetosphere, which acts as a huge shield. It protects the earth from the solar wind, a stream of electrically charged particles from the sun. Particles that get through the magnetosphere are trapped in the Van Allen belts.

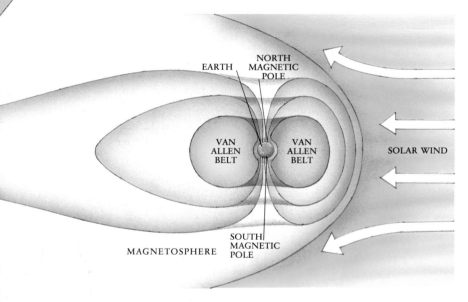

THE SEASONS AND DAYS

It takes a year for the earth to circle the sun. The earth is slightly tilted, so one half of the globe, or hemisphere, is closer to the sun than the other. This tilt causes the seasons. The hemisphere tilted towards the sun receives more heat, and so has summer, while the hemisphere that is tilted away has winter. As it circles the sun, the earth also spins on its axis, turning once every 24 hours. This rotation causes our days and nights. The side of the earth facing the sun has day, while the other side has night.

MARCH
Spring in the northern hemisphere.

DECEMBER
Summer in the southern hemisphere.

JUNE
Summer in the northern hemisphere.

SEPTEMBER
Spring in the southern hemisphere.

INSIDE THE EARTH

Scientists believe that the earth was formed about 4.6 billion years ago from a spinning cloud of gas and dust, which shrank to form a hot ball of liquid, or molten, rock. As it cooled, the earth's surface formed into a solid crust. Under the surface the temperature is so high that parts of the earth are still liquid. Movement of this molten material in the outer core is thought to produce the earth's magnetic fields.

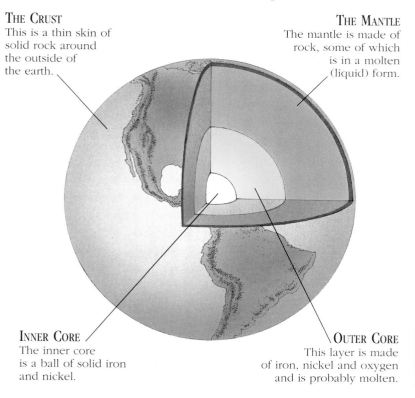

THE CRUST
This is a thin skin of solid rock around the outside of the earth.

THE MANTLE
The mantle is made of rock, some of which is in a molten (liquid) form.

INNER CORE
The inner core is a ball of solid iron and nickel.

OUTER CORE
This layer is made of iron, nickel and oxygen and is probably molten.

THE WANDERING CONTINENTS

The earth's crust is made up of pieces called plates, which float on top of a layer of molten rock in the mantle. There are seven main plates and several smaller ones. The magnetic forces within the earth move the plates slowly around the globe in an ever-changing jigsaw.

Geologists believe that about 270 million years ago all the land on earth was joined together in one "super-continent," which they call Pangaea. But, as the plates moved around, the land in this super-continent, slowly started to split up. This movement is called continental drift. The maps below show how geologists think the continents have moved and split apart to form the landmasses that we know today.

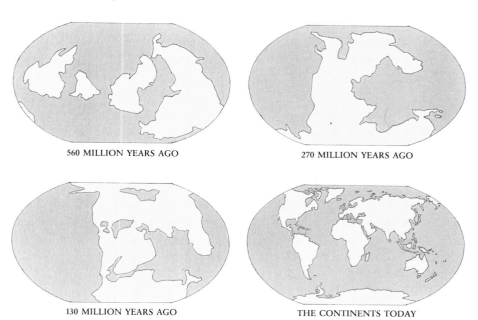

560 MILLION YEARS AGO

270 MILLION YEARS AGO

130 MILLION YEARS AGO

THE CONTINENTS TODAY

THE RESTLESS EARTH

As the plates move around the globe they collide, overlap, and slide past each other. The plates travel very slowly – their fastest speed is about 6 in (15 cm) in a year – but over millions of years the results of this movement can be dramatic. Huge mountain ranges, spectacular rift valleys, and deep trenches in the ocean bed have all been formed in areas where two

plates meet. Earthquakes, volcanoes, geysers and hot mud pools are also caused by plate movements. The regions in the world where they are found closely follow the joins between the plates.

SLIDING PAST
The San Andreas Fault in California is an example of a place where two plates are sliding past each other. The sliding movement often occurs in short bursts which are felt on the surface as earthquakes.

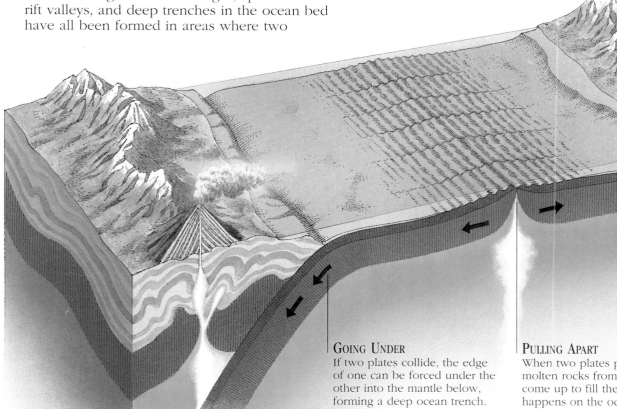

GOING UNDER
If two plates collide, the edge of one can be forced under the other into the mantle below, forming a deep ocean trench. The rocks from the crust melt in the mantle. Often these molten rocks force their way to the surface to form volcanoes.

PULLING APART
When two plates pull apart, molten rocks from the mantle come up to fill the gap. If this happens on the ocean floor it creates underwater mountain ridges. On land, it forms steep-sided valleys, such as the Great Rift Valley in East Africa.

COLLISION COURSE
Sometimes when two plates collide rocks are forced up to form great mountain ranges. These mountains are often volcanic. The Andes range in South America and the Himalayas in Asia were both formed by colliding plates.

CLIMATES AROUND THE WORLD

CLIMATE is the name given to the typical weather conditions and temperature in a particular area. Similar types of climate are found in different places around the world. For example, there are regions of hot, dry desert in Africa, North America, and central Australia.

The climate in any particular place depends partly on its latitude, that is, how far north or south of the equator it lies. The regions around the equator are the hottest places in the world. The further away from the equator you go, the colder the climate becomes. The coldest places in the world are the polar regions around the north and south poles.

Climate is also affected by how close a place is to the sea. The sea warms and cools the land near it, so coastal areas usually have fewer extremes of temperature than places in the center of a continent. Another important influence is altitude – how high a place is above sea level. The higher the place, the colder is its climate.

POLAR AND TUNDRA REGIONS
The areas round the north and south poles are covered in ice. The temperature only rises above freezing point for a few months of the year. South of the north pole lie regions known as the tundra, where the lower parts of the soil are permanently frozen and only mosses and lichens can grow. As the climate is very dry, the tundra regions are sometimes described as cold deserts.

During the short summer period, the edges of the polar ice caps melt. Large pieces of ice break off and form icebergs.

MOUNTAIN REGIONS
The temperature in mountainous regions varies a lot – the higher up you go, the colder it becomes. Trees and plants often grow on the lower slopes of mountains, but above a certain height (known as the tree line), temperatures are too low for vegetation to survive. Still higher up is the snow line. Above this it is so cold that the ground is permanently covered by snow and ice.

Mount Kilimanjaro in Kenya lies almost on the equator, but it is so high that its peak is covered in snow all year round.

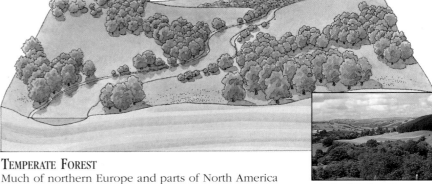

TAIGA
Taiga is a Russian word which means "cold forest." It is used to describe the huge areas of evergreen forest that stretch across northern parts of Canada, Scandinavia, and the USSR. Evergreen trees, such as spruces, pines and firs, are the only type of vegetation that can survive in the long, snowy winters and short summers of this type of climate.

The trees in the taiga regions are an important source of wealth. They are used for timber and for making paper.

TEMPERATE FOREST
Much of northern Europe and parts of North America have a temperate climate, which means that the temperature is never very hot or very cold. Because these regions have rainfall throughout the year, they were once covered by forests. Most of these have now been cut down. Deciduous trees, which shed their leaves in the winter, are common in temperate regions.

Much of the land in northern Europe has been cleared for farming, and small pockets of trees are all that is left of the forests.

THE OCEAN FLOOR

The ocean floor is not flat. Like the land, it has many geographical features, such as mountain ranges, flat plains and deep trenches. The longest range of mountains in the world is the underwater Indian Ocean–Pacific Ocean Cordillera. It stretches from East Africa, through the Indian Ocean, around southern Australia, and across the Pacific Ocean to the Gulf of California – a distance of 19,200 miles (30,900 km). The deepest point in the oceans, the Mariana trench in the Pacific Ocean near Japan, is about 36,201 ft (11,034 m) below sea level – deeper than the height of Mount Everest. The shallowest parts of the oceans are the areas of seabed around the edges of the continents, which are called the continental shelves.

Continental shelf　　　*Ocean trench*

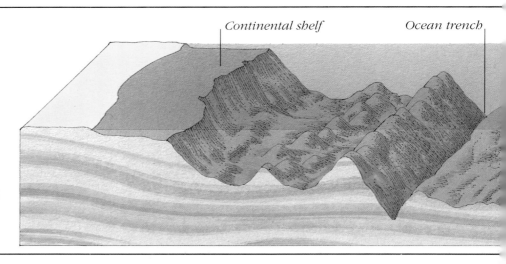

MEDITERRANEAN

The name "Mediterranean" is given to the type of climate which is found around the Mediterranean Sea, and in other similar regions of the world, such as California in North America. These areas have hot, dry summers and cool, wet winters. The trees and plants that grow there are specially adapted to survive the lack of water in summer.

Olive trees are one of the few plants that thrive in this climate. They have been cultivated around the Mediterranean for many centuries.

DRY GRASSLAND

In the middle of some of the continents are huge plains of grassland, such as the North American Prairies, the Russian Steppe, and the Argentinian Pampas. These regions have extreme climates – very hot summers and very cold winters. Large parts of these areas have now been taken over for farming and are used for growing wheat or raising cattle.

South American farmers raise large numbers of beef cattle on the grassy plains of the Pampas.

HOT DESERT

The hottest and driest climates in the world are found in the tropical deserts, such as the Sahara in Africa and the Australian Outback. The temperature there often reaches 100° F (38° C) in the shade. In some desert areas there may be no rain for several years. Deserts often contain sandy soil that can only support plants such as cacti, which are adapted to the dry conditions.

The dry, desert plains of the Australian Outback cover more than two-thirds of the continent. Few plants and animals can survive there.

TROPICAL GRASSLAND

Between the wet equatorial rain forests and the hot dry deserts lie regions of tropical grassland, such as the African Savannah. Here the climate is always hot, but the year divides between a dry and a wet season. Tall grasses and low trees and bushes grow in these areas. Tropical grasslands are grazed by large herds of plant-eating animals.

The African Savannah is the last place on earth where huge herds of grazing animals, such as zebras, gazelles, and wildebeest, still survive.

EQUATORIAL RAIN FOREST

In the regions around the equator, the climate is hot and wet all year round. The temperature remains constant at about 80–82° F (27–28° C). Vegetation thrives in this type of climate, and the equatorial regions used to be covered in dense rain forest. Much of this has now been cut down, although large areas still remain in the Amazon river basin in South America.

The Amazon rain forest covers an area 12 times the size of France. It is home to more species of birds and animals than anywhere else on earth.

WHERE CLIMATES ARE FOUND

Polar and tundra	Temperate forest	Hot desert
Mountain regions	Mediterranean	Tropical grassland
Taiga	Dry grassland	Rain forest

Mid-ocean ridge   Volcanic island

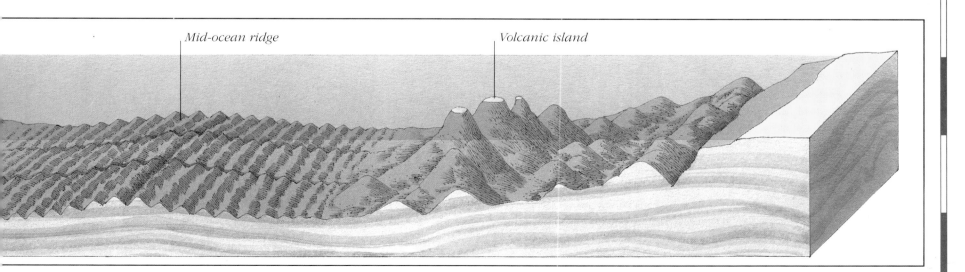

THE COUNTRIES OF THE WORLD

ALL OF THE CONTINENTS except Antarctica are divided into different countries, and these vary in size. By far the largest country in the world is the USSR, which stretches across two continents – Europe and Asia. The second largest country is Canada and the third largest is China. At the other end of the scale, the smallest country is the Vatican City, which lies in the city of Rome in Italy. It has a total area of only 0.17 sq mile (0.44 sq km). The USSR is more than 50 million times bigger than the Vatican City.

LATITUDE AND LONGITUDE

To help locate places in the world, geographers draw imaginary lines around the globe. Lines of latitude circle the globe from east to west. They are measured in degrees north or south of the equator. Lines of longitude circle the earth from north to south and are measured in degrees east or west of the line called the prime meridian.

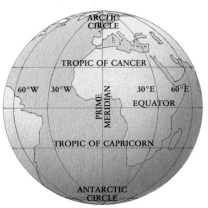

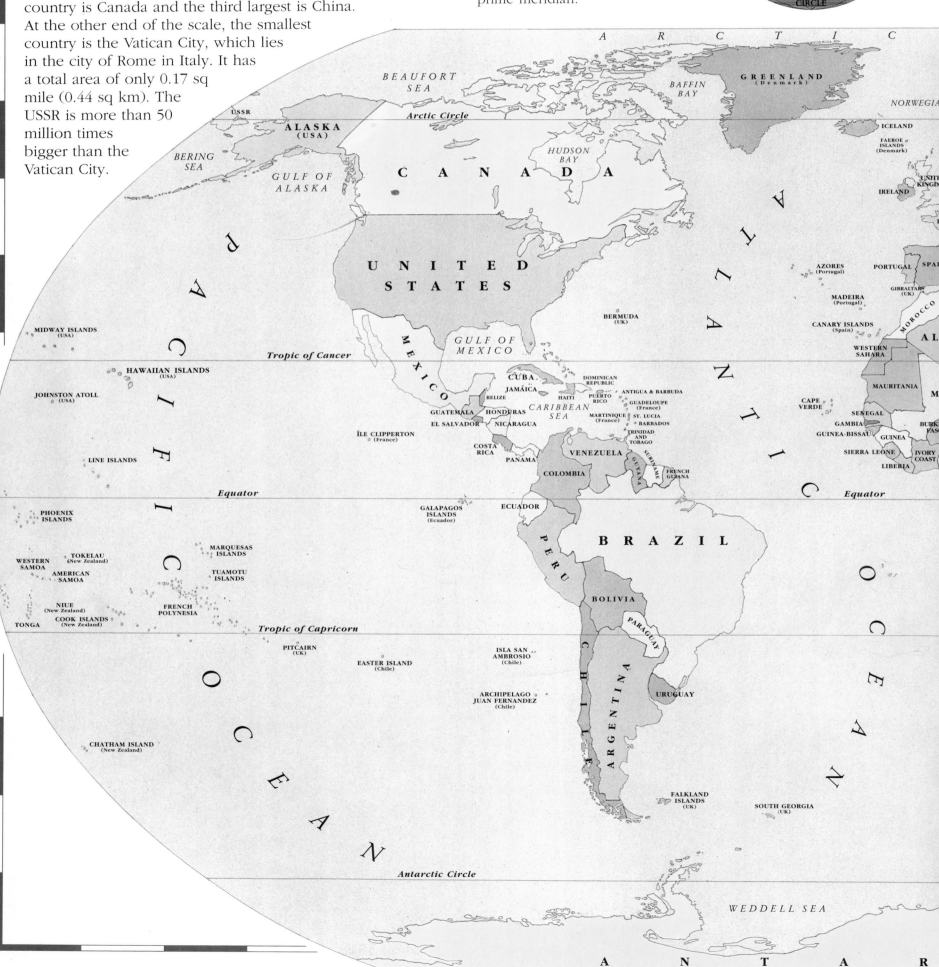

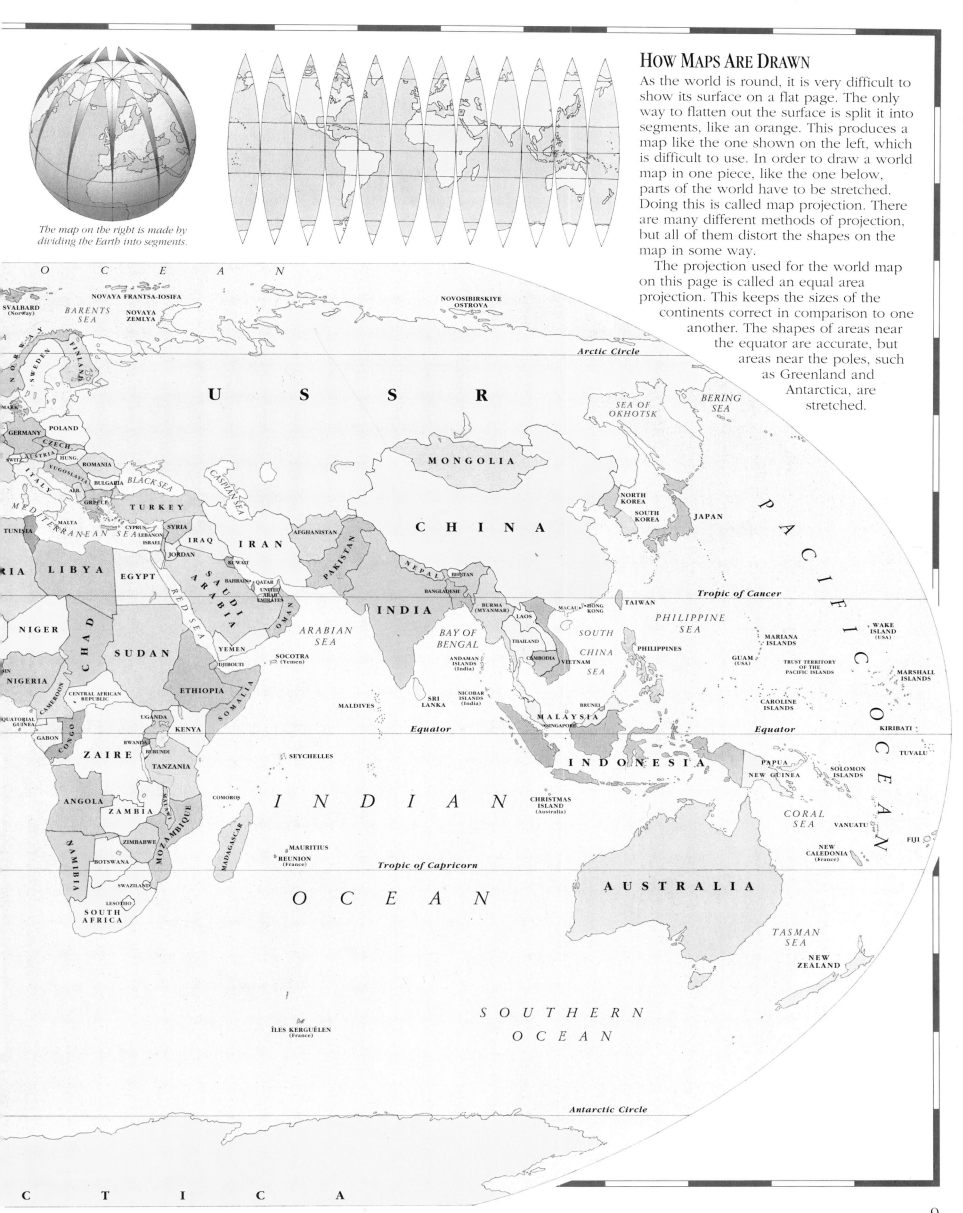

The map on the right is made by dividing the Earth into segments.

HOW MAPS ARE DRAWN

As the world is round, it is very difficult to show its surface on a flat page. The only way to flatten out the surface is split it into segments, like an orange. This produces a map like the one shown on the left, which is difficult to use. In order to draw a world map in one piece, like the one below, parts of the world have to be stretched. Doing this is called map projection. There are many different methods of projection, but all of them distort the shapes on the map in some way.

The projection used for the world map on this page is called an equal area projection. This keeps the sizes of the continents correct in comparison to one another. The shapes of areas near the equator are accurate, but areas near the poles, such as Greenland and Antarctica, are stretched.

THE BIGGEST, HIGHEST, AND LONGEST ON EARTH

WHAT IS THE LONGEST river on earth? How high is Mount Everest? Which is the world's biggest island? You can find the answers to all these questions below. Each of the sections is about one type of geographical feature – mountains, for example. The section contains the highest mountain on earth – Mount Everest – along with a selection of other mountains from around the world.

THE CONTINENTS

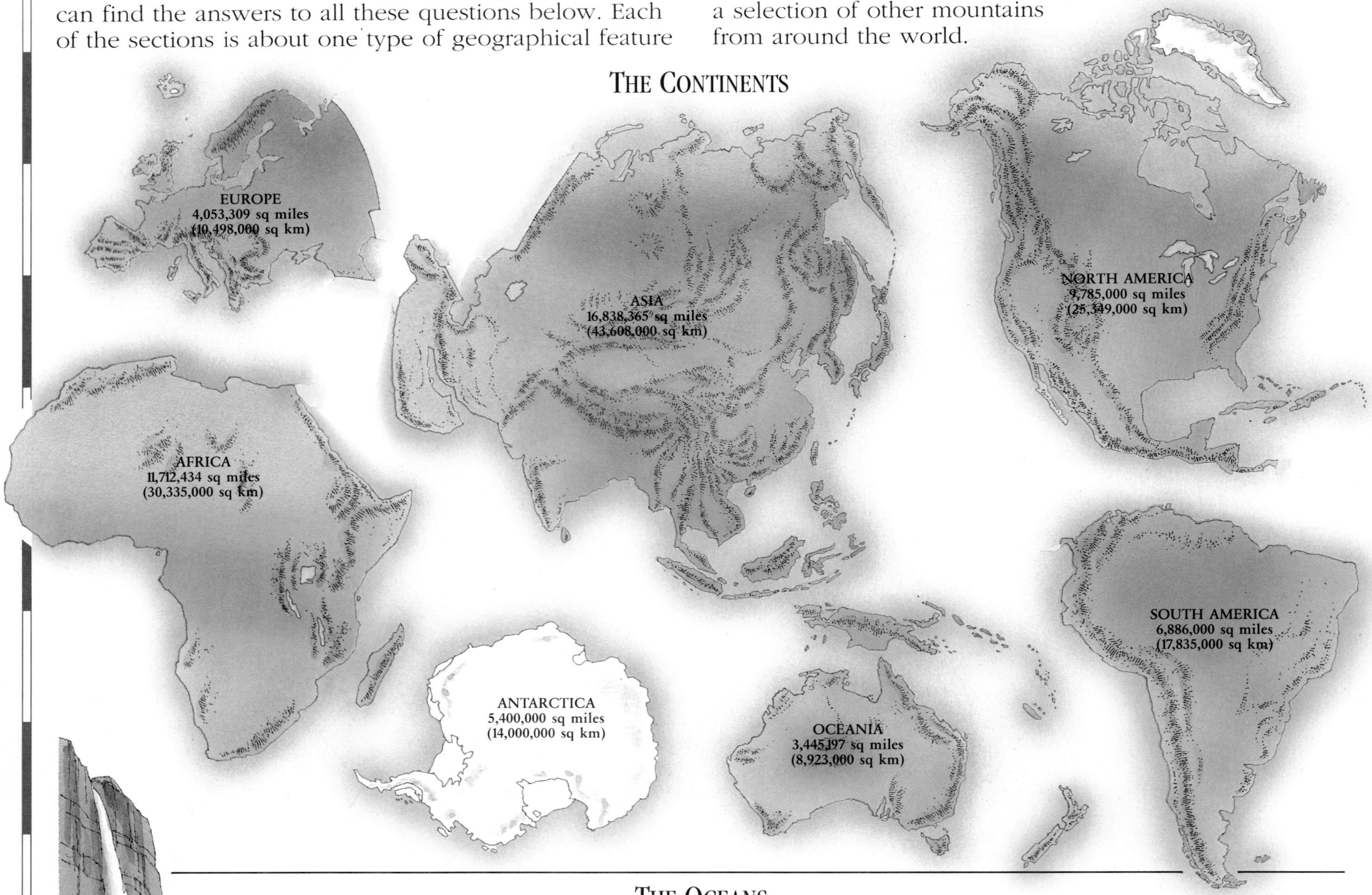

EUROPE
4,053,309 sq miles
(10,498,000 sq km)

ASIA
16,838,365 sq miles
(43,608,000 sq km)

NORTH AMERICA
9,785,000 sq miles
(25,349,000 sq km)

AFRICA
11,712,434 sq miles
(30,335,000 sq km)

SOUTH AMERICA
6,886,000 sq miles
(17,835,000 sq km)

ANTARCTICA
5,400,000 sq miles
(14,000,000 sq km)

OCEANIA
3,445,197 sq miles
(8,923,000 sq km)

THE OCEANS

ATLANTIC OCEAN
31,736,000 sq miles
(82,217,000 sq km)

INDIAN OCEAN
28,364,000 sq miles
(73,481,000 sq km)

PACIFIC OCEAN
63,838,000 sq miles
(165,384,000 sq km)

WATERFALLS

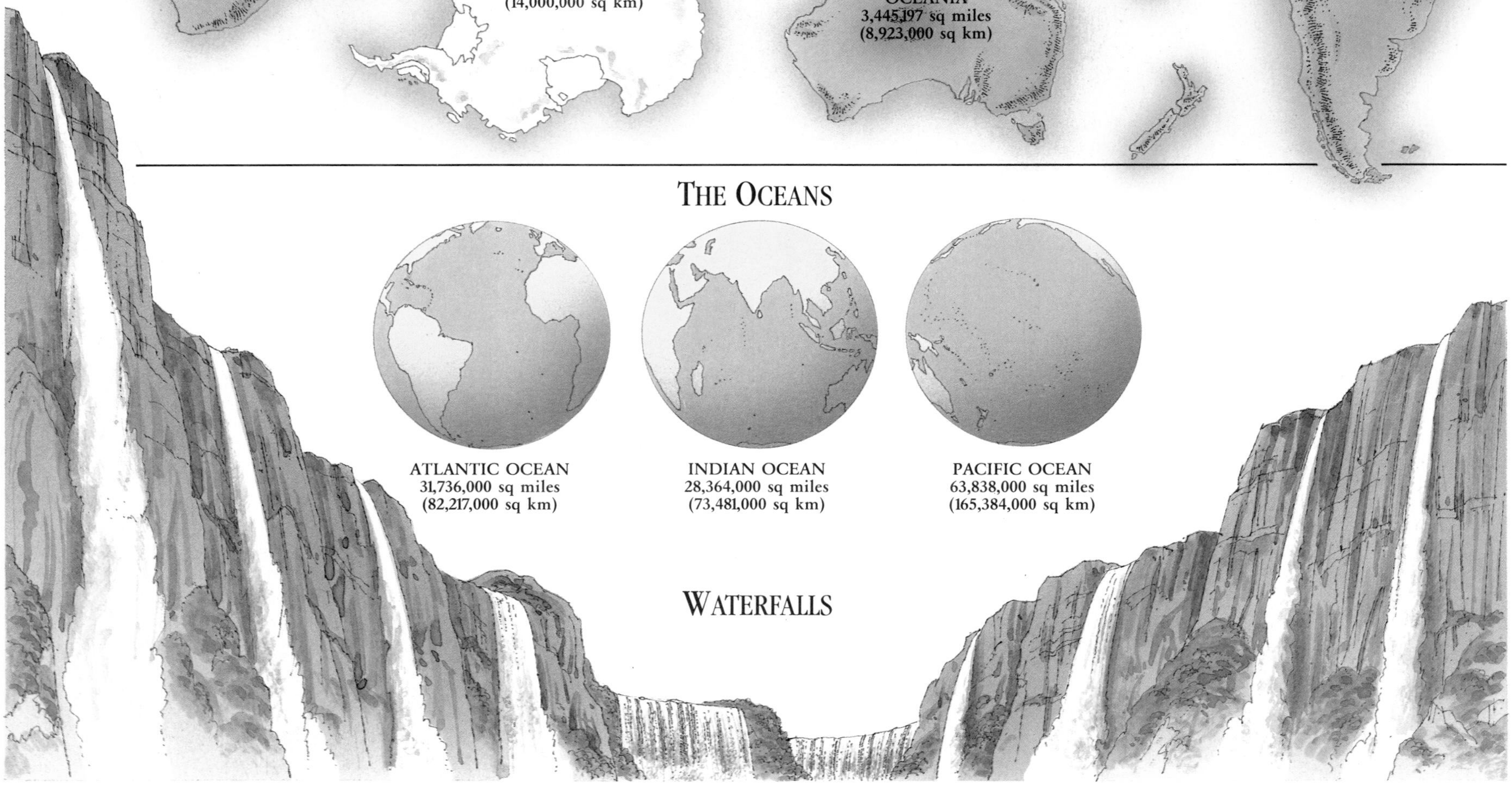

ANGEL	SUTHERLAND	GAVARNIE	JOG	VICTORIA	NIAGARA	FAIRY	VETTISFOSS	RIBBON	GIESSBACH
(Venezuela)	(New Zealand)	(France)	(India)	(Zambia-Zimbabwe)	(United States-Canada)	(United States)	(Norway)	(United States)	(Switzerland)
3,212 ft	1,904 ft	1,385 ft	830 ft	355 ft	182 ft	700 ft	900 ft	1,612 ft	1,982 ft
(979 m)	(580 m)	(422 m)	(253 m)	(108 m)	(55 m)	(213 m)	(274 m)	(491 m)	(604 m)

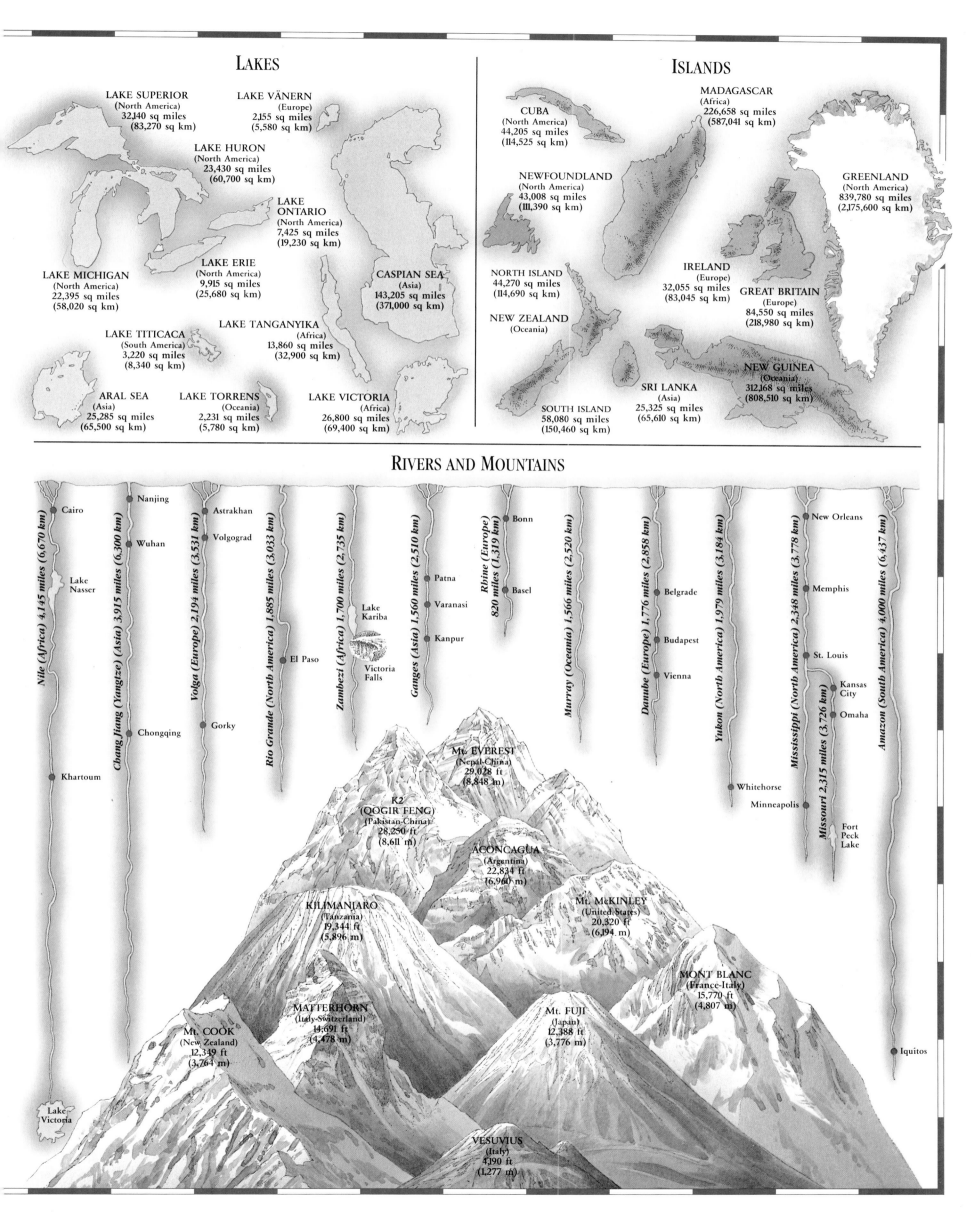

LAKES

LAKE SUPERIOR
(North America)
32,140 sq miles
(83,270 sq km)

LAKE VÄNERN
(Europe)
2,155 sq miles
(5,580 sq km)

LAKE HURON
(North America)
23,430 sq miles
(60,700 sq km)

LAKE ONTARIO
(North America)
7,425 sq miles
(19,230 sq km)

LAKE ERIE
(North America)
9,915 sq miles
(25,680 sq km)

CASPIAN SEA
(Asia)
143,205 sq miles
(371,000 sq km)

LAKE MICHIGAN
(North America)
22,395 sq miles
(58,020 sq km)

LAKE TITICACA
(South America)
3,220 sq miles
(8,340 sq km)

LAKE TANGANYIKA
(Africa)
13,860 sq miles
(32,900 sq km)

ARAL SEA
(Asia)
25,285 sq miles
(65,500 sq km)

LAKE TORRENS
(Oceania)
2,231 sq miles
(5,780 sq km)

LAKE VICTORIA
(Africa)
26,800 sq miles
(69,400 sq km)

ISLANDS

CUBA
(North America)
44,205 sq miles
(114,525 sq km)

MADAGASCAR
(Africa)
226,658 sq miles
(587,041 sq km)

NEWFOUNDLAND
(North America)
43,008 sq miles
(111,390 sq km)

GREENLAND
(North America)
839,780 sq miles
(2,175,600 sq km)

NORTH ISLAND
44,270 sq miles
(114,690 sq km)

NEW ZEALAND
(Oceania)

IRELAND
(Europe)
32,055 sq miles
(83,045 sq km)

GREAT BRITAIN
(Europe)
84,550 sq miles
(218,980 sq km)

SOUTH ISLAND
58,080 sq miles
(150,460 sq km)

SRI LANKA
(Asia)
25,325 sq miles
(65,610 sq km)

NEW GUINEA
(Oceania)
312,168 sq miles
(808,510 sq km)

RIVERS AND MOUNTAINS

Nile (Africa) 4,145 miles (6,670 km) — Cairo, Lake Nasser, Khartoum

Chang Jiang (Yangtze) (Asia) 3,915 miles (6,300 km) — Nanjing, Wuhan, Chongqing

Volga (Europe) 2,194 miles (3,531 km) — Astrakhan, Volgograd, Gorky

Rio Grande (North America) 1,885 miles (3,033 km) — El Paso

Zambezi (Africa) 1,700 miles (2,735 km) — Lake Kariba, Victoria Falls

Ganges (Asia) 1,560 miles (2,510 km) — Patna, Varanasi, Kanpur

Rhine (Europe) 820 miles (1,319 km) — Bonn, Basel

Murray (Oceania) 1,566 miles (2,520 km)

Danube (Europe) 1,776 miles (2,858 km) — Belgrade, Budapest, Vienna

Yukon (North America) 1,979 miles (3,184 km) — Whitehorse

Mississippi (North America) 2,348 miles (3,778 km) — New Orleans, Memphis, St. Louis, Kansas City, Omaha, Minneapolis

Missouri 2,315 miles (3,726 km) — Fort Peck Lake

Amazon (South America) 4,000 miles (6,437 km) — Iquitos

Mt. EVEREST
(Nepal-China)
29,028 ft
(8,848 m)

K2
(QOGIR FENG)
(Pakistan-China)
28,250 ft
(8,611 m)

ACONCAGUA
(Argentina)
22,834 ft
(6,960 m)

KILIMANJARO
(Tanzania)
19,344 ft
(5,896 m)

Mt. McKINLEY
(United States)
20,320 ft
(6,194 m)

MONT BLANC
(France-Italy)
15,770 ft
(4,807 m)

MATTERHORN
(Italy-Switzerland)
14,691 ft
(4,478 m)

Mt. FUJI
(Japan)
12,388 ft
(3,776 m)

Mt. COOK
(New Zealand)
12,349 ft
(3,764 m)

Lake Victoria

VESUVIUS
(Italy)
4,190 ft
(1,277 m)

WHERE PEOPLE LIVE

THE TOTAL POPULATION of the world is more than five billion people. Noone knows the exact figure, as it is constantly rising. The population of the world is growing faster now than ever before. It has doubled since 1950, and many experts believe that it will double again within the next 40 years.

The population of the world is not spread evenly around the globe. Many of the most densely populated countries are in Europe and Asia. In the Netherlands, for example, an average of 936 people live in each square mile of land. In contrast, Australia has an average of only five people per square mile.

POPULATION BY CONTINENT

The diagrams below show how many people live in each of the continents. Antarctica is the only continent which has no permanent population: the only people who live there are scientists and engineers.

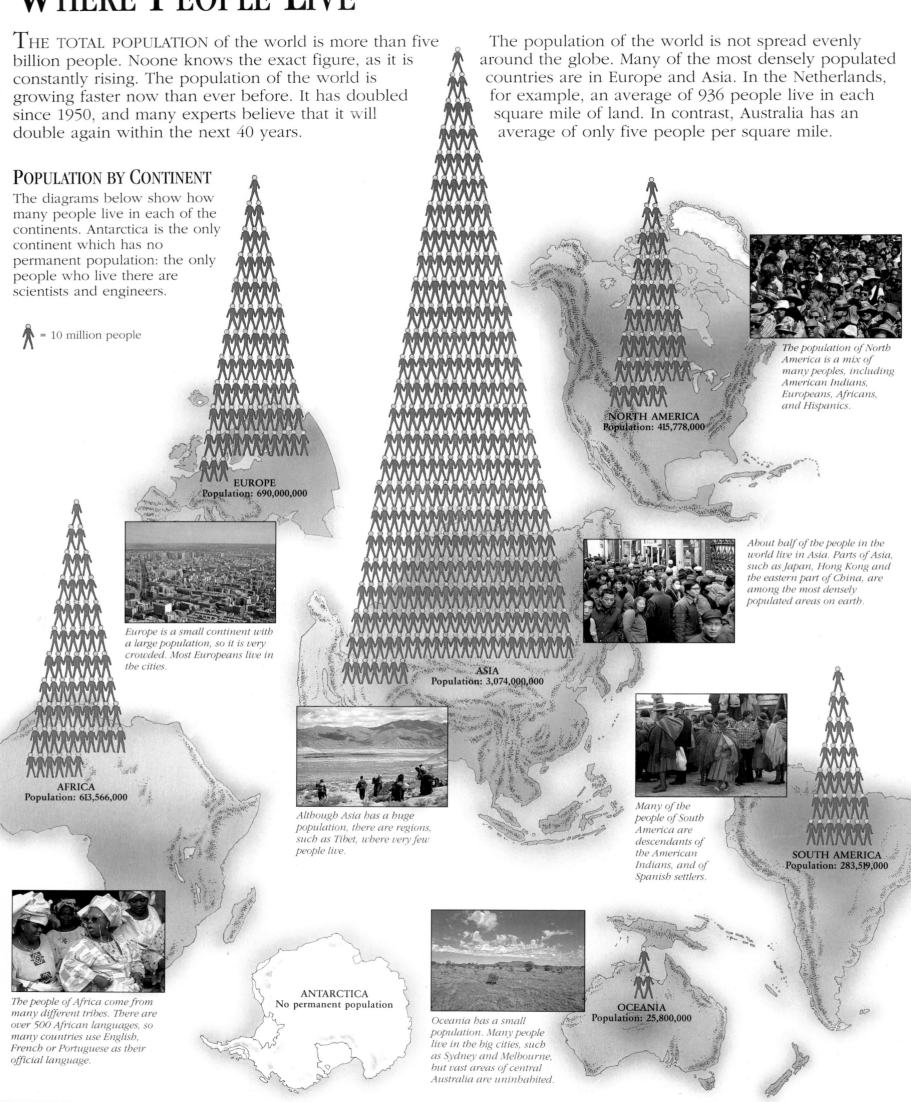

= 10 million people

EUROPE
Population: 690,000,000

Europe is a small continent with a large population, so it is very crowded. Most Europeans live in the cities.

AFRICA
Population: 613,566,000

The people of Africa come from many different tribes. There are over 500 African languages, so many countries use English, French or Portuguese as their official language.

ASIA
Population: 3,074,000,000

Although Asia has a huge population, there are regions, such as Tibet, where very few people live.

NORTH AMERICA
Population: 415,778,000

The population of North America is a mix of many peoples, including American Indians, Europeans, Africans, and Hispanics.

About half of the people in the world live in Asia. Parts of Asia, such as Japan, Hong Kong and the eastern part of China, are among the most densely populated areas on earth.

Many of the people of South America are descendants of the American Indians, and of Spanish settlers.

SOUTH AMERICA
Population: 283,519,000

ANTARCTICA
No permanent population

Oceania has a small population. Many people live in the big cities, such as Sydney and Melbourne, but vast areas of central Australia are uninhabited.

OCEANIA
Population: 25,800,000

How to Use This Atlas

The maps in this atlas are split into a number of sections. There is one section for each of the continents: Antarctica, North America, South America, Europe, Asia, Africa, and Oceania. At the start of each section is a map of the whole continent, like the one of North America shown at the bottom of this page. Following this are a series of regional maps, like the one of France below, which show all the countries in that continent. This page shows how to use these maps and explains what the symbols on the maps mean.

National Flags
The flags of all the countries on the map are shown like this.

Bordering Countries
Countries which lie around the edges of the area shown on the map are colored yellow.

Using the Grid
The grid around the outside of the page helps you to find places on the map. For example, to find the city of Paris, look its name up in the index on pages 77–80. Next to the word Paris are the reference numbers 39 E13. The first number shows that Paris is on page 39 of the atlas. The second number means that it is in square E13 of the grid. Turn to page 39. Trace across from the letter E on the grid and then down from the number 13. Paris is situated in the area where the two meet.

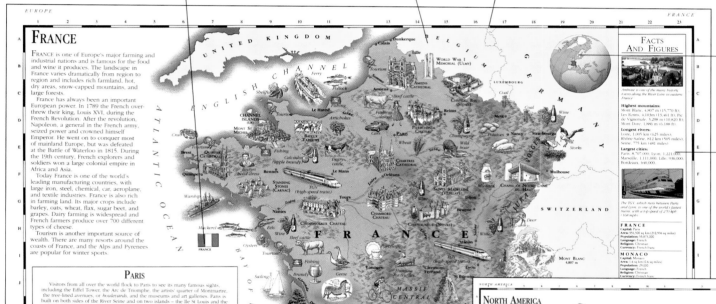

Where on Earth?
The red area on the globe shows where the countries on the map are situated.

Facts and Figures
This box contains interesting facts and statistics about each of the countries on the map.

Special Features
Features like this one give further information about a place or feature of interest on the map.

Scale
You can use the scale to see how big the countries are, and how far it is from one place to another. Not all the maps have been drawn to the same scale.

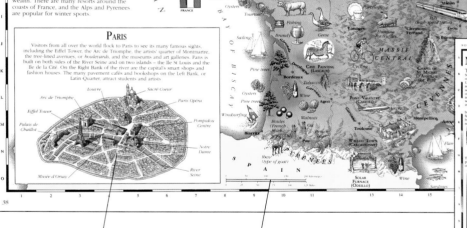

Political Map
This shows all the countries in the continent.

Geographical Map
This map of the continent shows all the main geographical features, such as rivers, mountains, lakes and deserts.

Key to the Maps

Capital City	City	Country name	Range of mountains	An individual mountain with its height	River	Lake	A specific building or place	A product, animal, plant or activity that is found all over the region
• **LONDON**	• **Bristol**	F R A N C E	*A L P S*	△ **Mt. Everest** 29,028 ft	*Ganges*	*LAKE TITICACA*	**The Leaning Tower of Pisa**	*Wine*

THE ARCTIC

THE ARCTIC CIRCLE contains the northernmost parts of North America, Europe and Asia, along with most of the island of Greenland. The temperature in the Arctic is so low that much of the Arctic Ocean is permanently frozen. Within the Arctic Circle, there are days in midwinter when the sun never rises, and days in midsummer when it never sets. Despite the harsh climate, a wide variety of animals and plants live in the Arctic. The main human inhabitants are the Inuit (Eskimos) and the Sami (Lapps).

The island of Greenland is anything but green – much of it is permanently covered by ice. The Inuit have lived in Greenland since about 2500 B.C. The first Europeans to settle there were the Vikings, in about A.D. 986. Today Greenland is a self-governing province of Denmark.

FACTS AND FIGURES

Flowing river of ice, called a glacier, in Greenland.

Highest mountain:
Mt. Gunnbjorn (Greenland), 12,139 ft (3,700 m).

Beneath the North Pole:
There is no solid land. This was proved in 1958 when a submarine, the USS Nautilus, traveled under the ice.

Flight Paths over the Arctic:
These provide the shortest air connections between Europe and North America.

GREENLAND
Area: 839,780 sq miles (2,175,600 sq km)
Population: 55,000

Kittiwake
Ptarmigan
Elk
ARCTIC CIRCLE (approx. 66.5° North)
BERING STRAIT
ALASKA
Moose
Evenk (Eskimo)
CHUKCHI SEA
Chukchi (Eskimo)
NORTHERN LIMIT OF FOREST
U
Polar bear
Snowy owl
Gray whale
Larga seal
Reindeer
Arctic tern
Caribou
Glaucous gull
Lemmings
S
Arctic fox
BANKS ISLAND
Long-tailed skua
Polar bear
I
B
Snow geese
Musk oxen
Arctic tern
ARCTIC OCEAN
White whale
Ermine
E
Skua
Eskimo with reindeer
+ **NORTH MAGNETIC POLE**
Robert Peary (USA) claimed he was the first person to reach the North Pole in 1909.
SEVERNAYA ZEMLYA
Brent goose
Arctic wolves
R
Arctic fox
○ NORTH POLE
Arctic tern
Polar bear
Arctic hares
I
Inuit (Eskimo)
Long-tailed skua
A
HUDSON BAY
Polar bear
Bearded seal
Barnacle goose
N
Snow goose
Inuit (Eskimo)
BAFFIN ISLAND
NOVAYA ZEMLYA
Walruses
BAFFIN BAY
Ptarmigan
Lemmings
Ringed seal
Guillemots
Nenet (Eskimo)
Narwhals
Polar bear
Walrus
Walrus
C
Fishing trawler
Coal
SVALBARD ISLANDS
Right whale
Elk
A
Musk oxen
Barnacle goose
Killer whale
BARENTS SEA
Great black-backed gulls
Guillemots
GREENLAND (DENMARK)
Hooded seal
Gray seals
MT. GUNNBJORN 12,139 ft
MT. FOREL 11,000 ft
Harp seals
Cod
Puffins
Humpback whale
Ringed seal
Lapp with reindeer
LAPLAND
LIMIT OF PERMANENT PACK ICE
ICELAND
Sperm whale

0 200 400 600 800 Kilometers
0 125 250 375 500 Miles

THE ANTARCTIC

THE ANTARCTIC has the coldest and harshest climate in the world. Nearly all the land is covered by ice, on average about 6,562 ft (2,000 m) thick. The size of the ice sheet varies between the seasons. In summer the ice at the edge of the sheet melts or breaks off to form icebergs. In winter the sea at the edge of the ice sheet freezes again and is called pack ice. There are very few plants. The animals that live in the Antarctic, such as seals and penguins, depend on the sea for their supply of food.

Although no country owns Antarctica, a number of countries claim territory, and many have bases there for scientific research. Even the small population of scientists dwindles during the bitter Antarctic winter, when blizzards last for days. The world's coldest temperature of -128.6°F (-89.2°C) was recorded at Vostok Station in July 1983.

FACTS AND FIGURES

The sea around the Antarctic is covered by drifting pack ice for most of the year.

Antarctica contains 90 per cent of all the world's ice: If it melted, the level of the seas throughout the world would rise by 200 ft (60 m) and drown all the coastal towns and cities.

CONTINENT OF ANTARCTICA
Area: 5,400,000 sq miles (14,000,000 sq km)
Inhabitants: Scientists and engineers only
Climate: Cold, dry and windy

Imperial shags
Gentoo penguins
Antarctic cod
Chinstrap penguins
Piked whale
Crabeater seals
Elephant seals
Snow petrels
Toothfish
Krill
Crabeater seal
Antarctic fulmar
Ross seal
Blue whale
South polar skua
Iceberg
Tourist liner
Leopard seal
Ross seal
Fin whale

Elephant seals
Giant petrel
Survey ship

ANTARCTIC CIRCLE (approx. 66.5° South)

SOUTH ATLANTIC OCEAN

Iceberg
Right whale
Antarctic petrels
Crabeater seal

WEDDELL SEA

Adélie penguins

Emperor penguins
HALLEY STATION (UK)

Emperor penguins
RONNE ICE SHELF

Survey plane

MARIE BYRD LAND

AMUNDSEN-SCOTT STATION (USA)

ANTARCTICA

South Pole

Roald Amundsen (Norway) first reached South Pole December 1911.

Adélie penguins

+ SOUTH MAGNETIC POLE

Robert Scott (UK) reached South Pole January 1912.

ROSS ICE SHELF

VOSTOK STATION (USSR)

McMURDO AIR STATION (USA)

Emperor penguins

Snow petrels

Adélie penguins

Chinstrap penguins

DUMONT D'URVILLE STATION (France)

WILKES LAND

CASEY BASE (Australia)

QUEEN MAUD LAND

Fish factory ship
Humpback whale

Antarctic fulmars

Leopard seal

Emperor penguins

South polar skua

MOLODEZHNAYA STATION (USSR)

Weddell seal

Emperor penguins

Antarctic petrels

Elephant seals

Snow petrels

Adélie penguins

Krill

Antarctic cod

Killer whale

Leopard seal

Ice fish

INDIAN OCEAN

SOUTH PACIFIC OCEAN

AMUNDSEN SEA

BELLINGSHAUSEN SEA

LIMIT OF PERMANENT PACK ICE

NORTH AMERICA

TWO LARGE COUNTRIES, Canada and the United States of America, take up more than three-quarters of the continent of North America. South of the United States lies the country of Mexico and the region called Central America, which contains seven small countries. The Caribbean islands lie off the southeast coast of the continent. These islands are often called the West Indies. Greenland, which lies northeast of Canada, is the largest island in the world.

Mountain scenery, Alberta, Canada.

The western side of the continent is dominated by the Rocky Mountains. East of the Rockies lie the fertile farmlands of the American Great Plains, drained by two great rivers, the Mississippi and Missouri. To the north of the Great Plains, much of Canada is covered by vast regions of pine forest. The northernmost part of the continent lies within the Arctic Circle.

Ancient Maya city of Palenque, Mexico.

The first settlers crossed to North America from Asia in 40,000 B.C., when Alaska was joined to Siberia by a land bridge. These people were the ancestors of the American Indians.

The first Europeans to discover the continent were probably the Vikings in about A.D. 1000, but Europeans only began to settle there in the 16th century. Over the next 200 years the British gained control of much of northern North America, while the Spanish took over Central America.

Between 1775 and 1783 colonists fought the American Revolution to break free of British control and subsequently set up the country that is now the United States. Canada became an independent country in 1867.

Millions of people emigrated to North America from Europe in search of a better life. For 300 years the Europeans also shipped black slaves from Africa to provide labor on their farms in the Caribbean and the southern states. Today the people of North America are a mix from many lands. English is the common language in the United States and most of Canada (although some Canadians speak French), while Spanish is spoken in Mexico and most of Central America.

The Capitol Building, Washington DC, United States.

FACTS ABOUT NORTH AMERICA

Area: 9,785,000 sq miles (25,349,000 sq km).

Population: 415,778,000.

Number of independent countries: 23.

Largest countries: Canada, 3,851,809 sq miles (9,976,169 sq km); United States, 3,614,363 sq miles (9,363,123 sq km); Mexico, 761,530 sq miles (967,183 sq km).

Most populated countries: United States, 245,871,000; Mexico, 83,593,000.

Largest cities: New York City (United States), 16,800,900; Mexico City (Mexico), 14,100,000; Los Angeles (United States), 9,763,600; Chicago (United States), 7,717,100.

Longest rivers: Mississippi-Missouri, 3,740 miles (6,019 km); Mackenzie, 2,635 miles (4,240 km); Yukon, 1,979 miles (3,184 km).

Highest mountains: Mt. McKinley (United States), 20,320 ft (6,194 m); Mt. Logan (Canada), 19,524 ft (5,951 m).

Largest lakes: Lake Superior (United States), 32,140 sq miles (83,270 sq km); Lake Huron (United States), 23,430 sq miles (60,700 sq km); Great Bear Lake (Canada), 12,270 sq miles (31,790 sq km).

Largest islands: Greenland, 839,780 sq miles (2,175,600 sq km); Baffin Island, 183,760 sq miles (476,070 sq km).

Hottest place: Death Valley in California (United States) is the hottest place in North America. In 1917 the temperature there reached 120°F (48.9°C).

World's shortest river: The Roe River, which flows into the Missouri near Great Falls in Montana (United States), is only 200 ft (61 m) long.

World's highest geyser: Steamboat Geyser in Yellowstone National Park (United States) can reach 380 ft (115 m).

World's longest frontier: The border between Canada and the United States measures 3,987 miles (6,416 km).

13   14   15   16   17   18   19   20   21   22   23

A

B

C

D

ASIA

EUROPE

ARCTIC OCEAN

GREENLAND

ELLESMERE ISLAND

BAFFIN BAY

ATLANTIC

BERING STRAIT

BEAUFORT SEA

BANKS ISLAND

DAVIS STRAIT

BERING SEA

BROOKS RANGE

Yukon

VICTORIA ISLAND

BAFFIN ISLAND

LABRADOR SEA

△ MT. McKINLEY 20,320 ft

MACKENZIE MTS

GREAT BEAR LAKE

HUDSON BAY

KODIAK ISLAND

GULF OF ALASKA

Mackenzie

△ MT. LOGAN 19,524 ft

GREAT SLAVE LAKE

NEWFOUNDLAND

LAKE ATHABASCA

QUEEN CHARLOTTE ISLANDS

ROCKY

LAKE WINNIPEG

VANCOUVER ISLAND

Fraser

LAKE MANITOBA

LAKE HURON

St. Lawrence

LAKE ONTARIO

CAPE COD

OCEAN

PACIFIC

LAKE SUPERIOR

G R E A T

MTS

P L A I N S

LAKE MICHIGAN

LAKE ERIE

APPALACHIAN MTS

GREAT BASIN

GREAT SALT LAKE

Missouri

Colorado

Mississippi

SIERRA MADRE OCCIDENTAL

Rio Grande

GULF OF CALIFORNIA

SIERRA MADRE ORIENTAL

△ CITLALTEPETL 18,700 ft

GULF OF MEXICO

LESSER ANTILLES

GREATER   ANTILLES

YUCATAN PENINSULA

GULF OF HONDURAS

CARIBBEAN SEA

SOUTH

LAKE NICARAGUA

AMERICA

O   C   E   A   N

L

M

N

O

13   14   15   16   17   18   19   20   21   22   23

CANADA AND ALASKA

CANADA is the world's second largest country, yet its population is small – only about one-tenth the size of the smaller United States, its southern neighbor. More than half of all Canadians live in the area around the Great Lakes and the St. Lawrence river. In the center of Canada lie the Prairies, a flat plain used mainly for grazing cattle and growing wheat. Northern Canada is covered by vast areas of forest and tundra, while the west of the country is dominated by the Rocky Mountains.

The first inhabitants of Canada were the Indian and Inuit (Eskimo) peoples. French and British settlers started to move

there in the 17th century. Although Canada became part of the British Empire, the French influence has always been strong and many Canadians still speak French today. Canada became an independent country in 1867.

Alaska, which lies to the northwest of Canada, is the largest state in the United States. Alaska is one of the world's major oil-producing regions.

MONTREAL

Montreal, situated in the province of Quebec, is one of Canada's largest cities. Two-thirds of the people in Montreal speak French, making it the second largest French-speaking city in the world after Paris. French traders founded the city, which they called Ville-Marie, in 1642. It was built on Montreal Island on the St. Lawrence river. Today, Montreal is Canada's leading port and a major trading and manufacturing center.

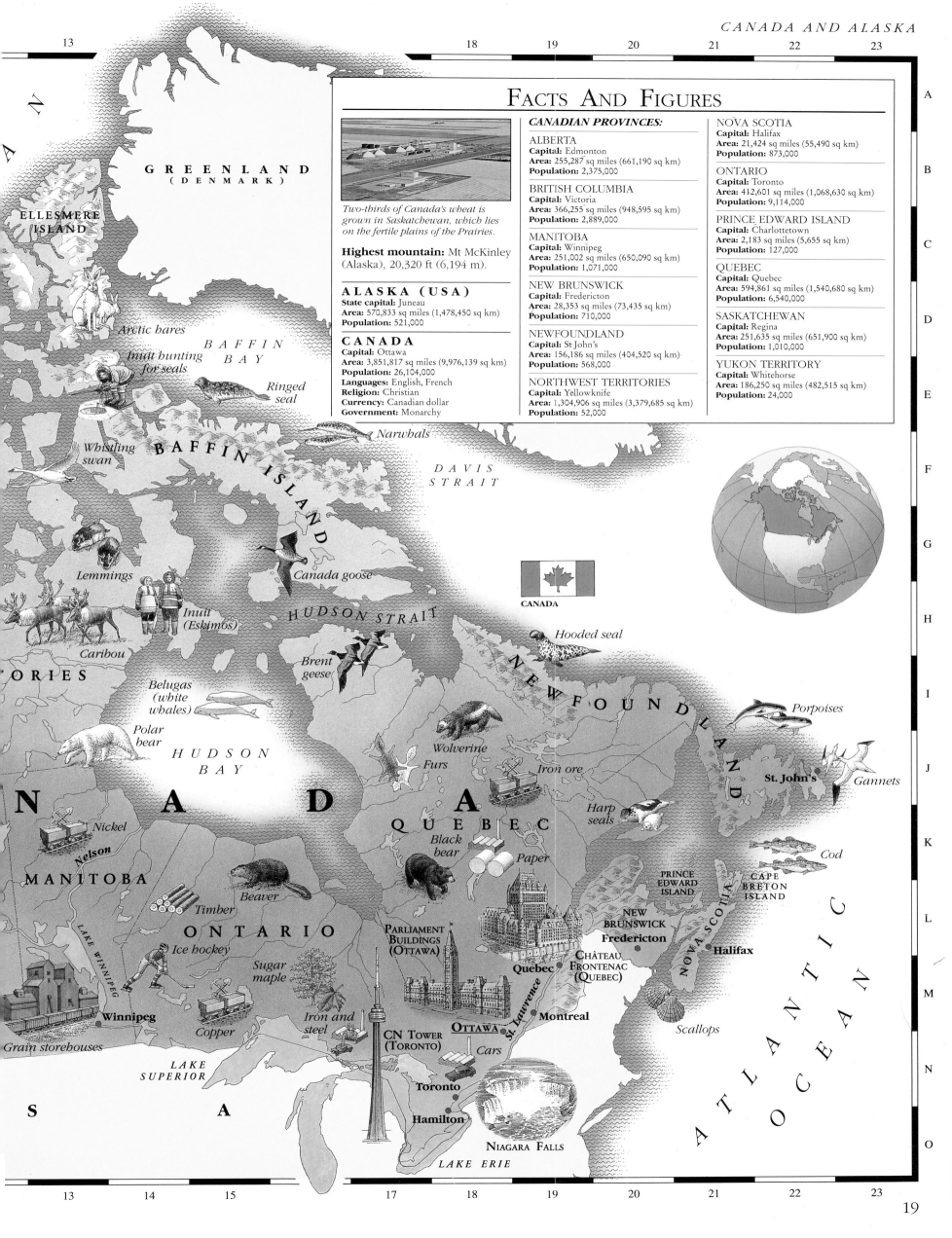

FACTS AND FIGURES

Two-thirds of Canada's wheat is grown in Saskatchewan, which lies on the fertile plains of the Prairies.

Highest mountain: Mt McKinley (Alaska), 20,320 ft (6,194 m).

ALASKA (USA)
State capital: Juneau
Area: 570,833 sq miles (1,478,450 sq km)
Population: 521,000

CANADA
Capital: Ottawa
Area: 3,851,817 sq miles (9,976,139 sq km)
Population: 26,104,000
Languages: English, French
Religion: Christian
Currency: Canadian dollar
Government: Monarchy

CANADIAN PROVINCES:

ALBERTA
Capital: Edmonton
Area: 255,287 sq miles (661,190 sq km)
Population: 2,375,000

BRITISH COLUMBIA
Capital: Victoria
Area: 366,255 sq miles (948,595 sq km)
Population: 2,889,000

MANITOBA
Capital: Winnipeg
Area: 251,002 sq miles (650,090 sq km)
Population: 1,071,000

NEW BRUNSWICK
Capital: Fredericton
Area: 28,353 sq miles (73,435 sq km)
Population: 710,000

NEWFOUNDLAND
Capital: St John's
Area: 156,186 sq miles (404,520 sq km)
Population: 568,000

NORTHWEST TERRITORIES
Capital: Yellowknife
Area: 1,304,906 sq miles (3,379,685 sq km)
Population: 52,000

NOVA SCOTIA
Capital: Halifax
Area: 21,424 sq miles (55,490 sq km)
Population: 873,000

ONTARIO
Capital: Toronto
Area: 412,601 sq miles (1,068,630 sq km)
Population: 9,114,000

PRINCE EDWARD ISLAND
Capital: Charlottetown
Area: 2,183 sq miles (5,655 sq km)
Population: 127,000

QUEBEC
Capital: Quebec
Area: 594,861 sq miles (1,540,680 sq km)
Population: 6,540,000

SASKATCHEWAN
Capital: Regina
Area: 251,635 sq miles (651,900 sq km)
Population: 1,010,000

YUKON TERRITORY
Capital: Whitehorse
Area: 186,250 sq miles (482,515 sq km)
Population: 24,000

CANADA

Map labels:

GREENLAND (DENMARK)

ELLESMERE ISLAND

Arctic hares

Inuit hunting for seals

BAFFIN BAY

Ringed seal

Whistling swan

BAFFIN ISLAND

Narwhals

DAVIS STRAIT

Lemmings

Canada goose

Inuit (Eskimos)

Caribou

HUDSON STRAIT

Hooded seal

NEWFOUNDLAND

Brent geese

Porpoises

Belugas (white whales)

Polar bear

HUDSON BAY

Wolverine

Furs

Iron ore

St. John's

Gannets

N A D A

QUEBEC

Harp seals

Cod

Nickel

Black bear

Paper

PRINCE EDWARD ISLAND

CAPE BRETON ISLAND

Nelson

MANITOBA

Beaver

Timber

ONTARIO

Ice hockey

Sugar maple

Parliament Buildings (Ottawa)

Château Frontenac (Quebec)

Quebec

NEW BRUNSWICK

Fredericton

NOVA SCOTIA

Halifax

Winnipeg

Copper

Iron and steel

CN Tower (Toronto)

Ottawa

Montreal

St. Lawrence

Cars

Scallops

Grain storehouses

LAKE SUPERIOR

LAKE WINNIPEG

Toronto

ATLANTIC OCEAN

S

A

Hamilton

NIAGARA FALLS

LAKE ERIE

THE UNITED STATES

THE UNITED STATES OF AMERICA is one of the largest and richest countries in the world. It is made up of 50 states, each of which has its own government. The national government is based in the capital, Washington DC. The letters "DC" stand for District of Columbia, the name of the area in which the city is situated.

The country is dominated by two mountain ranges – the Rockies in the west and the Appalachians in the east. In between lie the flat, fertile Great Plains, which are used for farming. The United States is rich in natural resources. It has large deposits of raw materials, such as iron, coal, and oil, which are needed to produce industrial goods. These resources have helped the country to become the world's greatest industrial manufacturer. The United States is also rich in farmland, and exports large amounts of agricultural produce, especially cereals, cotton, and tobacco. Most years, the United States exports more grain than all the other countries of the world combined.

The United States is often described as a "melting pot" because its population is a mix of many peoples. The country's first inhabitants were the American Indians. Later, settlers came from all over Europe, especially the UK, Italy, Ireland, and Poland. The United States' black population are the descendants of slaves who were brought to America from Africa. More recent arrivals include Hispanics (Spanish-speakers) from Mexico and South America, and Asians.

THE NORTHEASTERN STATES

THE NORTHEASTERN part of the United States is the most crowded region in the country. Large numbers of people live along the Atlantic coast in the big cities of Boston, New York City, Philadelphia, Baltimore, and Washington. This coast was the first area of the United States to be settled by Europeans. In 1620 colonists from England, who are known as the "Pilgrims," established the first settlement at New Plymouth, Massachusetts, in the region that is still called New England.

Farther inland lie the Great Lakes, the largest group of freshwater lakes in the world, which form part of the border between the United States and Canada. The region around the Great Lakes has the greatest concentration of industry in the United States. The biggest cities are Chicago, Pittsburgh, and Detroit, which is known as the "Motor City" because it is the center of the American car industry. The main products of the area are iron and steel, machinery, cars, chemicals, coal, and textiles.

West and southwest of the Great Lakes are the states of Minnesota, Wisconsin, and Iowa, which lie on the flat land of the Great Plains. Much of the United States' wheat and corn is grown in this area, which is often called the "farm belt".

FACTS AND FIGURES

The area of New England is famous for its spectacular forests and old wooden houses.

THE UNITED STATES
Capital: Washington DC
Area: 3,618,794 sq miles (9,372,614 sq km)
Population: 245,871,000
Language: English
Religion: Christian
Currency: US dollar
Government: Republic

UNITED STATES

NEW YORK CITY

The skyline of Manhattan Island in the center of New York City is perhaps the best-known view of any city in the world. It was the first sight of America for the millions of people who emigrated there from Europe during the 19th and early 20th centuries. Today, New York is the largest city in the United States, the country's leading port, and a world financial center.

FACTS AND FIGURES

The skyline of Chicago is dominated by the Sears Tower – the world's tallest building.

THE NORTHEASTERN STATES:

CONNECTICUT
Capital: Hartford
Area: 4,872 sq miles (12,620 sq km)
Population: 3,174,000

DELAWARE
Capital: Dover
Area: 1,932 sq miles (5,005 sq km)
Population: 622,000

ILLINOIS
Capital: Springfield
Area: 55,645 sq miles (144,120 sq km)
Population: 11,535,000

INDIANA
Capital: Indianapolis
Area: 35,932 sq miles (93,065 sq km)
Population: 5,499,000

IOWA
Capital: Des Moines
Area: 55,965 sq miles (144,950 sq km)
Population: 2,884,000

KENTUCKY
Capital: Frankfort
Area: 39,668 sq miles (102,740 sq km)
Population: 3,679,000

MAINE
Capital: Augusta
Area: 30,994 sq miles (80,275 sq km)
Population: 1,164,000

MARYLAND
Capital: Annapolis
Area: 9,837 sq miles (25,480 sq km)
Population: 4,392,000

MASSACHUSETTS
Capital: Boston
Area: 7,824 sq miles (20,265 sq km)
Population: 5,822,000

MICHIGAN
Capital: Lansing
Area: 56,957 sq miles (147,520 sq km)
Population: 9,088,000

MINNESOTA
Capital: St Paul
Area: 79,548 sq miles (206,030 sq km)
Population: 4,193,000

MISSOURI
Capital: Jefferson City
Area: 68,944 sq miles (178,565 sq km)
Population: 5,029,000

NEW HAMPSHIRE
Capital: Concord
Area: 8,992 sq miles (23,290 sq km)
Population: 998,000

NEW JERSEY
Capital: Trenton
Area: 7,467 sq miles (19,340 sq km)
Population: 7,562,000

NEW YORK
Capital: Albany
Area: 47,376 sq miles (122,705 sq km)
Population: 17,783,000

OHIO
Capital: Columbus
Area: 41,004 sq miles (106,200 sq km)
Population: 10,744,000

PENNSYLVANIA
Capital: Harrisburg
Area: 44,888 sq miles (116,260 sq km)
Population: 11,853,000

RHODE ISLAND
Capital: Providence
Area: 1,054 sq miles (2,730 sq km)
Population: 968,000

VERMONT
Capital: Montpelier
Area: 9,613 sq miles (24,900 sq km)
Population: 535,000

VIRGINIA
Capital: Richmond
Area: 39,695 sq miles (102,835 sq km)
Population: 5,387,000

WASHINGTON DC
Area: 63 sq miles (163 sq km)
Population: 626,000

WEST VIRGINIA
Capital: Charleston
Area: 24,119 sq miles (62,470 sq km)
Population: 1,936,000

WISCONSIN
Capital: Madison
Area: 54,427 sq miles (140,965 sq km)
Population: 4,775,000

C A N A D A

St. Lawrence

White pine

Potatoes

Blueberries

M A I N E

Augusta

Skiing

GULF OF MAINE

VERMONT
Montpelier

NEW HAMPSHIRE

FORT TICONDERAGA

Concord

Sugar maple

THE STATE HOUSE OF BOSTON

NEW YORK

Skiing

Albany

Boston

MASSACHUSETTS

CAPE COD

LAKE HURON

LAKE ONTARIO

NIAGARA FALLS

Hartford
CONNECTICUT

RHODE ISLAND

Providence

Cars

LAKE ST. CLAIR

LAKE ERIE

THE STATUE OF LIBERTY

New York City

LONG ISLAND

Tourism

Lansing
Detroit

Cleveland

Iron and steel

Oil

PENNSYLVANIA

Chemicals

Trenton
NEW JERSEY

Ocean liner

Iron and steel

Soy beans

Akron

Coal

Harrisburg

Tires

Pittsburgh

Philadelphia

O H I O

Amish people

Baltimore

Tourism

Columbus

Strip-mining coal

THE CAPITOL BUILDING

Annapolis

Dover
DELAWARE

DELAWARE BAY

WASHINGTON DC

Baseball

Cincinnati

WEST VIRGINIA

Mackerel

Ohio

Charleston

MARYLAND

CHESAPEAKE BAY

Frankfort

Chemicals

Richmond

KENTUCKY

Coal

V I R G I N I A

Warship

THE NATURAL BRIDGE

The Kentucky Derby

Tobacco

Peanuts

N O R T H   C A R O L I N A

A T L A N T I C   O C E A N

APPALACHIAN MTS

Scale:
0 100 200 300 400 500 Kilometers
0 50 100 150 200 250 300 Miles

THE SOUTHERN STATES

THE SOUTHERN STATES, which are often just called "the South", extend from the Atlantic coast in the east to the Mexican border in the west. Flowing southwards through the region is the Mississippi River, which reaches the Gulf of Mexico at New Orleans. Before the railways were built, the Mississippi was North America's most important trading route.

In the 18th and 19th centuries, the wealth of the South was based on farming. Cotton, tobacco, and other crops were grown on large farms called plantations. The workers on the plantations were black slaves, who were brought over from Africa. In the 1860s a civil war was fought in America between the southern states (the Confederacy) and the northern states (the Union). One of the main causes of the war was that the South refused to get rid of slavery. In 1865, the Union was victorious and the slaves were freed.

In the west of this region lies the huge state of Texas, which is famous for its cattle ranches and its oil. The long peninsula of Florida, in the southeast, is popular for vacations and attracts tourists from all over the world because of its good climate and beautiful beaches.

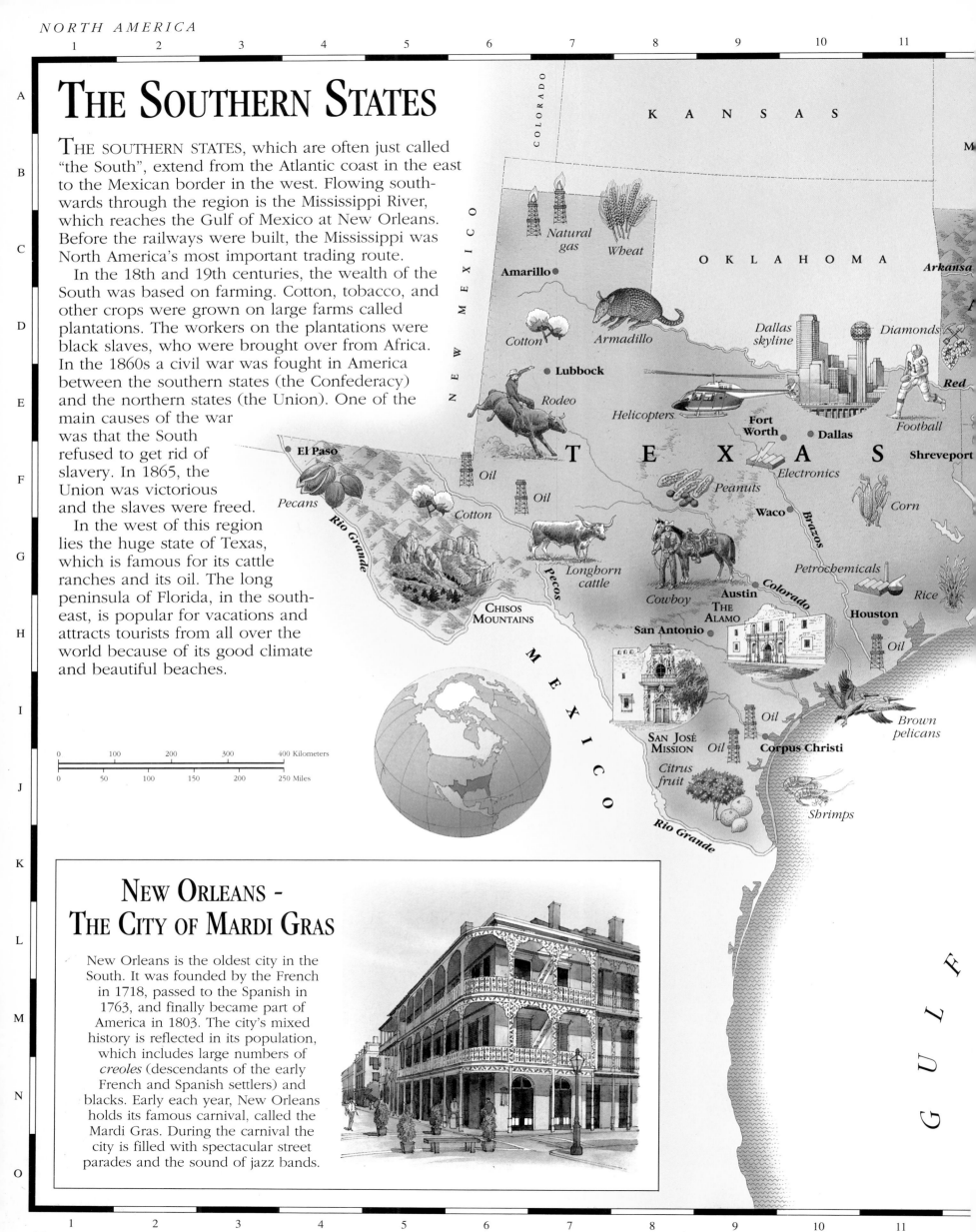

KANSAS

COLORADO

NEW MEXICO

OKLAHOMA

Arkansa

Natural gas

Wheat

Amarillo

Cotton *Armadillo*

Dallas skyline *Diamonds*

Lubbock

Rodeo

Red

Helicopters

Fort Worth **Dallas**

Football

TEXAS

Shreveport

El Paso

Oil *Oil* *Peanuts* *Electronics* *Corn*

Pecans

Cotton **Waco** *Brazos*

Rio Grande

Longhorn cattle *Petrochemicals* *Rice*

Pecos *Cowboy* **Austin** *Colorado*

CHISOS MOUNTAINS THE ALAMO **Houston**

San Antonio *Oil*

MEXICO

Oil

Brown pelicans

SAN JOSÉ MISSION *Oil* **Corpus Christi**

Citrus fruit

Shrimps

Rio Grande

GULF

| 0 | 100 | 200 | 300 | 400 Kilometers |
| 0 | 50 | 100 | 150 | 200 | 250 Miles |

NEW ORLEANS - THE CITY OF MARDI GRAS

New Orleans is the oldest city in the South. It was founded by the French in 1718, passed to the Spanish in 1763, and finally became part of America in 1803. The city's mixed history is reflected in its population, which includes large numbers of *creoles* (descendants of the early French and Spanish settlers) and blacks. Early each year, New Orleans holds its famous carnival, called the Mardi Gras. During the carnival the city is filled with spectacular street parades and the sound of jazz bands.

ILLINOIS

INDIANA

SSOURI

KENTUCKY

WEST VIRGINIA

VIRGINIA

Soy beans

Catfish

Cotton

Country and western music

Nashville

Knoxville

Poultry

Textiles

Tobacco

Greensboro

Raleigh

First powered flight by the Wright brothers

T E N N E S S E E

N O R T H   C A R O L I N A

Dairy cattle

Chattanooga

Charlotte

Sweet potatoes

RKANSAS

Memphis

Tennessee

Black bear

Textiles

Little Rock

Rice

Oil

M I S S I S S I P P I

Iron and steel

Coca Cola

S O U T H   C A R O L I N A

Columbia

Tobacco

Magnolia tree

Atlanta

CONFEDERATE MEMORIAL (STONE MT)

Savannah

Charleston

Shrimps

Mississippi steamer

A L A B A M A

G E O R G I A

Soy beans

Birmingham

Columbus

Cotton

Savannah

Jackson

Cotton

Paper

Jazz music

L O U I S I A N A

Montgomery

Alabama

Raccoon

Cotton

Peanuts

Flint

Water-melons

Pearl

Oil

Palmetto tree

Yellowtail snapper

Oil

Oil

Mobile

Chattahoochee

Tallahassee

Jacksonville

Tourism

Baton Rouge

F L O R I D A

New Orleans

MISSISSIPPI DELTA

Shrimps

Cruiser

THE EPCOT CENTER (DISNEY WORLD)

Orlando

CAPE CANAVERAL (SPACE LAUNCH SITE)

Oil

Alligator

Oysters

Lobster

Tampa

A T L A N T I C   O C E A N

Oil rig

THE EVERGLADES

BAHAMAS

Tourism

G U L F   O F   M E X I C O

Anhinga (diving bird)

Fort Lauderdale

Miami

FLORIDA KEYS

FACTS AND FIGURES

The city of Miami in Florida is a popular tourist resort. Many Americans retire there.

Largest cities: Miami (Florida), 2,827,300; Houston (Texas), 2,755,100; Dallas-Fort Worth (Texas), 2,727,300; Atlanta (Georgia), 1,962,500; New Orleans (Louisiana), 1,185,000.

Longest river: Mississippi, 2,348 miles (3,778 km).

World's largest theme park: Disney World, in Florida, covers an area of 44 sq miles (113 sq km). It had over 22 million visitors in 1988.

THE SOUTHERN STATES:

ALABAMA
Capital: Montgomery
Area: 50,766 sq miles (131,485 sq km)
Population: 4,021,000

ARKANSAS
Capital: Little Rock
Area: 52,077 sq miles (134,880 sq km)
Population: 2,359,000

FLORIDA
Capital: Tallahassee
Area: 54,152 sq miles (140,255 sq km)
Population: 11,366,000

GEORGIA
Capital: Atlanta
Area: 58,056 sq miles (150,365 sq km)
Population: 5,976,000

LOUISIANA
Capital: Baton Rouge
Area: 44,521 sq miles (115,310 sq km)
Population: 4,481,000

MISSISSIPPI
Capital: Jackson
Area: 47,233 sq miles (122,335 sq km)
Population: 2,613,000

NORTH CAROLINA
Capital: Raleigh
Area: 48,843 sq miles (126,505 sq km)
Population: 6,255,000

SOUTH CAROLINA
Capital: Columbia
Area: 30,202 sq miles (78,225 sq km)
Population: 3,347,000

TENNESSEE
Capital: Nashville
Area: 41,154 sq miles (106,590 sq km)
Population: 4,762,000

TEXAS
Capital: Austin
Area: 262,017 sq miles (678,620 sq km)
Population: 16,370,000

The state of Texas is famous for its huge cattle ranches, where cowboys still round up the animals on horseback.

THE WESTERN STATES

THE WESTERN part of the United States has the most rugged landscape in the country, with high mountains, deserts, and river canyons. The Rocky Mountains, which dominate the states of Idaho, Montana, Wyoming, and Colorado, mark where the West begins. The early settlers struggled across this difficult countryside in their wagon trains, but it was not until the railways were built during the mid-1800s that the American West was opened up.

California is situated on the Pacific coast and has the largest population of any of the American states. The first Europeans to settle there were the Spanish, as can be seen from many of the place names, such as Los Angeles, San Francisco, and San Diego. The central valley of California contains some of the richest farming land in the country. California lies on the San Andreas Fault, where two parts of the earth's crust are slowly moving in different directions. This movement causes frequent earthquakes.

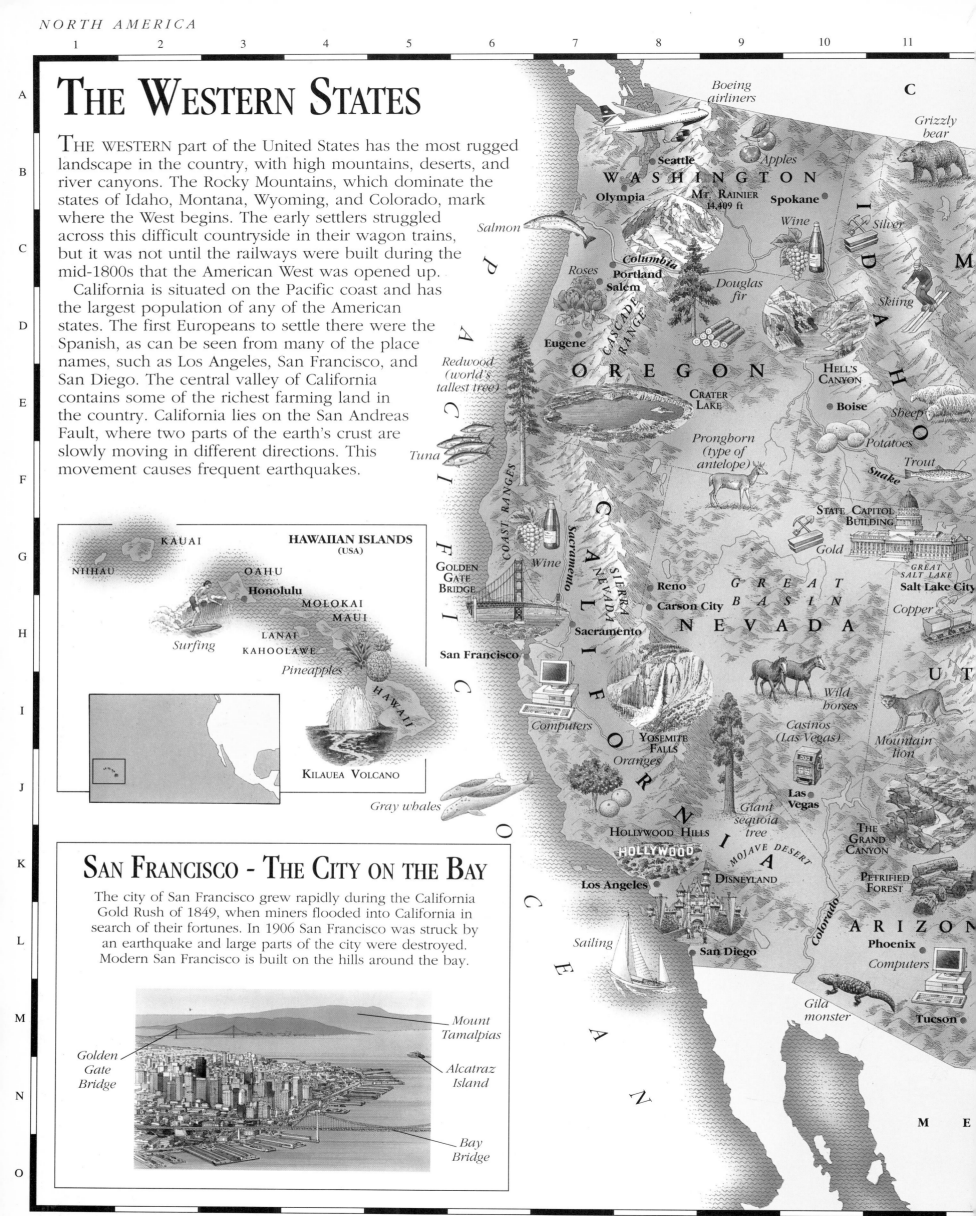

HAWAIIAN ISLANDS (USA)

KAUAI
NIHHAU
OAHU
Honolulu
MOLOKAI
MAUI
LANAI
KAHOOLAWE
Surfing
Pineapples
HAWAII
Kilauea Volcano

SAN FRANCISCO - THE CITY ON THE BAY

The city of San Francisco grew rapidly during the California Gold Rush of 1849, when miners flooded into California in search of their fortunes. In 1906 San Francisco was struck by an earthquake and large parts of the city were destroyed. Modern San Francisco is built on the hills around the bay.

Golden Gate Bridge
Mount Tamalpias
Alcatraz Island
Bay Bridge

Boeing airliners
Grizzly bear
Seattle
Apples
WASHINGTON
Olympia
MT. RAINIER 14,409 ft
Spokane
Salmon
Wine
Silver
Skiing
Columbia
Roses
Portland
Salem
Douglas fir
IDAHO
Eugene
HELL'S CANYON
OREGON
Redwood (world's tallest tree)
CRATER LAKE
Boise
Sheep
Potatoes
Pronghorn (type of antelope)
Snake
Trout
Tuna
STATE CAPITOL BUILDING
GREAT SALT LAKE
Gold
Salt Lake City
GOLDEN GATE BRIDGE
Wine
Reno
GREAT BASIN
Carson City
NEVADA
Copper
Sacramento
UT
San Francisco
Wild horses
Computers
Casinos (Las Vegas)
Mountain lion
Yosemite Falls
Oranges
Giant sequoia tree
Las Vegas
THE GRAND CANYON
Gray whales
Hollywood Hills
HOLLYWOOD
MOJAVE DESERT
PETRIFIED FOREST
Los Angeles
DISNEYLAND
ARIZON
Sailing
Phoenix
Computers
San Diego
Colorado
Gila monster
Tucson

PACIFIC
CALIFORNIA
COAST RANGES
SIERRA NEVADA
CASCADE RANGE
OCEAN

C A N A D A

Harvesting
wheat

Oil

Wild ducks

N O R T H

Oil

D A K O T A

Grand
Forks

Missouri

Great Falls

Oil

Bismarck

Wheat

Helena

OLD FAITHFUL
GEYSER
(YELLOWSTONE
NATIONAL PARK)

Yellowstone

Oil

Strip-mining
for coal

Sunflowers

M O N T A N A

DEVIL'S
TOWER

S O U T H

D A K O T A

Wapiti
(type of elk)

Pierre

Beef
cattle

GANNETT
PEAK
13,802 ft

Beef cattle

MT
RUSHMORE

Prairie dog

W Y O M I N G

Soy
beans

Coyote
(type of
wild dog)

N E B R A S K A

Cowboy

Wheat

Omaha

Cheyenne

Lincoln

Skiing

CHIMNEY
ROCK

Denver

Denver
skyline

BUFFALO BILL'S
RANCH HOUSE

Kansas
City

C O L O R A D O

K A N S A S

Topeka

RAINBOW
BRIDGE

Aircraft
industry

Oil

Indian
eagle dancer

MONUMENT
ROCKS

Wichita

SHIP ROCK

Rattlesnake

Oil

Sorghum
(cereal
crop)

Saguaros
(giant
cacti)

Cotton

Oil

Tulsa

Santa
Fe

Beef
cattle

N E W   M E X I C O

Albuquerque

Oklahoma City

Bison

O K L A H O M A

SOCORRO
SPACE
TELESCOPE

Corn

Rio Grande

T E X A S

CARLSBAD
CAVERNS

SAN
XAVIER
DE BAC
MISSION

M E X I C O

C A N A D A

M I N N E S O T A

I O W A

Missouri

M I S S O U R I

A R K A N S A S

0   100   200   300   400   500 Kilometers

0   100   200   300 Miles

MIDDLE AMERICA

CENTRAL AMERICA is a narrow land bridge that joins the two continents of North and South America. At its narrowest point, in Panama, a canal 51 miles (82 km) long has been built to join the Atlantic and Pacific Oceans. There are seven small countries in Central America. To the north of it lies Mexico and to the east lie the hundreds of islands of the Caribbean Sea, which are often called the West Indies. This is a region of great variety and contrasts – large and small, rich and poor, old and new – with a fascinating mixture of different cultures and troubled histories. Modern Mexico City, one of the largest cities in the world, lies on the site of an ancient city called Tenochtitlán, which was once the capital of the Aztec civilization.

On the Caribbean islands, tourist luxury and local poverty lie side by side. In the 16th century the islands were colonized by the Europeans, who shipped black slaves from Africa to work on the farms. Today the population is a mixture of many peoples. The main languages are English, Spanish, and dialects called *patois*, which are mixtures of African and French or English.

There are also great contrasts in the climate and vegetation of this area, from the Mexican desert in the north to the rain forests of the south, and the clear blue waters and coral islands in the east. Sometimes great tropical storms called hurricanes rage through the usually calm waters of the Caribbean. Winds of over 100 mph (160 kph) and enormous waves cause much damage.

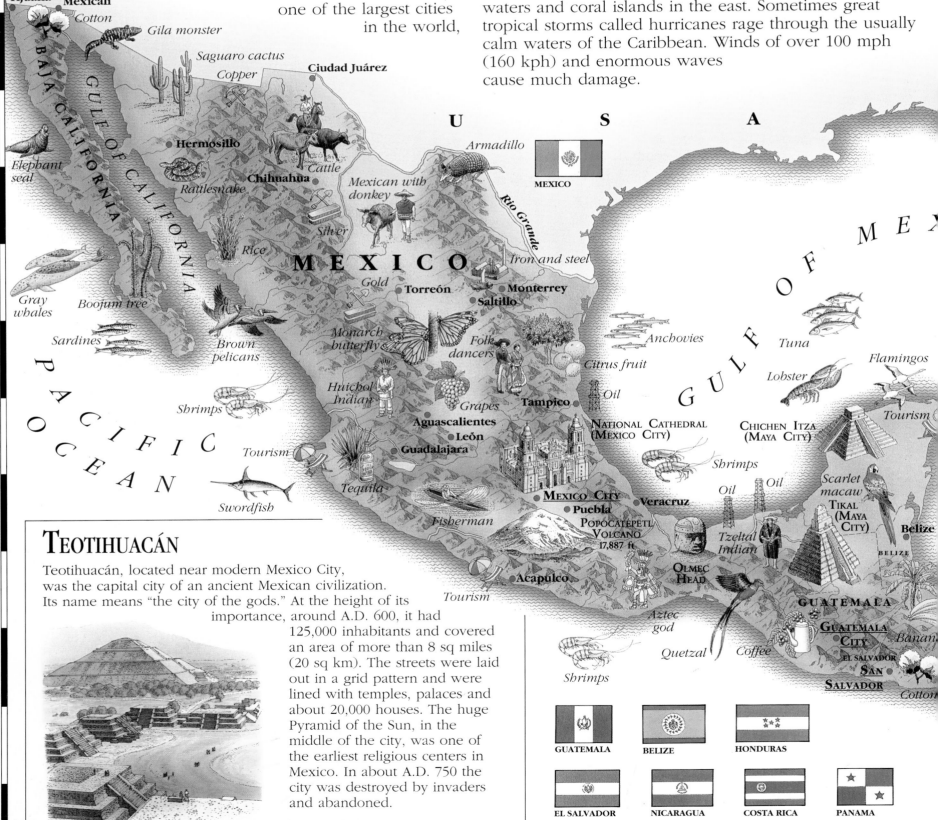

Tijuana
Mexicali
Cotton
Gila monster
Saguaro cactus
Copper
Ciudad Juárez
BAJA CALIFORNIA
GULF OF CALIFORNIA
Elephant seal
Hermosillo
Cattle
Armadillo
MEXICO
U S A
Rattlesnake
Chihuahua
Mexican with donkey
Rio Grande
Gray whales
Boojum tree
Silver
Rice
M E X I C O
Gold
Torreón
Monterrey
Saltillo
Iron and steel
GULF OF MEX
Sardines
Brown pelicans
Monarch butterfly
Folk dancers
Anchovies
Tuna
Flamingos
Huichol Indian
Citrus fruit
Lobster
Shrimps
Grapes
Tampico
Oil
GULF OF MEX
Tourism
Aguascalientes
León
Guadalajara
NATIONAL CATHEDRAL (MEXICO CITY)
CHICHEN ITZA (MAYA CITY)
Tourism
Tequila
Swordfish
Fisherman
MEXICO CITY
Puebla
Veracruz
POPOCATÉPETL VOLCANO 17,887 ft
Shrimps
Oil
Oil
Scarlet macaw
TIKAL (MAYA CITY)
Belize
BELIZE
Acapulco
OLMEC HEAD
Tzeltal Indian
Aztec god
Quetzal
Coffee
GUATEMALA
GUATEMALA CITY
Banan
EL SALVADOR
SAN SALVADOR
Cotton
Shrimps
Tourism
PACIFIC OCEAN
MEXICO

TEOTIHUACÁN

Teotihuacán, located near modern Mexico City, was the capital city of an ancient Mexican civilization. Its name means "the city of the gods." At the height of its importance, around A.D. 600, it had 125,000 inhabitants and covered an area of more than 8 sq miles (20 sq km). The streets were laid out in a grid pattern and were lined with temples, palaces and about 20,000 houses. The huge Pyramid of the Sun, in the middle of the city, was one of the earliest religious centers in Mexico. In about A.D. 750 the city was destroyed by invaders and abandoned.

GUATEMALA
BELIZE
HONDURAS
EL SALVADOR
NICARAGUA
COSTA RICA
PANAMA

13 14 15 16 17 18 19 20 21 22 23

A T L A N T I C   O C E A N

U · S · A

FACTS AND FIGURES

Jamaica, which means "island of springs", is a popular tourist resort.

World's fastest population growth: The population of Central America has more than tripled since 1900.

ANTIGUA & BARBUDA
Capital: St John's

ARUBA
Capital: Oranjestad

BAHAMAS
Capital: Nassau

BARBADOS
Capital: Bridgetown

BELIZE
Capital: Belmopan

COSTA RICA
Capital: San José

CUBA
Capital: Havana

DOMINICA
Capital: Roseau

DOMINICAN REPUBLIC
Capital: Santo Domingo

EL SALVADOR
Capital: San Salvador

GRENADA
Capital: St George's

GUADELOUPE
Capital: Basse Terre

GUATEMALA
Capital: Guatemala City

HAITI
Capital: Port-au-Prince

HONDURAS
Capital: Tegucigalpa

JAMAICA
Capital: Kingston

MARTINIQUE
Capital: Fort-de-France

MEXICO
Capital: Mexico City

NETHERLANDS ANTILLES
Capital: Willemstad

NICARAGUA
Capital: Managua

PANAMA
Capital: Panama City

PUERTO RICO
Capital: San Juan

ST. KITTS-NEVIS
Capital: Basseterre

ST. LUCIA
Capital: Castries

ST. VINCENT & THE GRENADINES
Capital: Kingstown

TRINIDAD & TOBAGO
Capital: Port-of-Spain

BAHAMAS   PUERTO RICO   BARBADOS   GRENADA   TRINIDAD & TOBAGO

CUBA   JAMAICA   HAITI   DOMINICAN REPUBLIC

Tourism

BAHAMAS

NASSAU

Cruise liner

Straits of Florida

Scuba diver

Sugarcane

HAVANA

Coral reefs

Coffee

TURKS & CAICOS ISLANDS (UK)

Cocoa

C U B A

Pineapples

Cigars

HAITI

PORT-AU-PRINCE

DOMINICAN REPUBLIC

SANTO DOMINGO

Coral reefs

Tourism

Frigate bird

ANGUILLA (UK)

VIRGIN ISLANDS (USA/UK)

ST. KITTS-NEVIS

ANTIGUA & BARBUDA

SAN JUAN

PUERTO RICO (US)

MONTSERRAT (UK)

Sailing

GUADELOUPE (Fr)

Coconuts

DOMINICA

MARTINIQUE (Fr)

Scuba diver

CAYMAN ISLANDS (UK)

JAMAICA

KINGSTON

Reggae music

Rum

Sharks

ST. LUCIA

BARBADOS

ST. VINCENT & THE GRENADINES

Green turtle

Nutmeg and mace

GRENADA

Steel bands

C A R I B B E A N   S E A

Grapefruit

HONDURAS

Cattle

TEGUCIGALPA

Coffee

TRINIDAD & TOBAGO

ARUBA (Neth)

NETHERLANDS ANTILLES

NICARAGUA

Bananas

Coffee

MANAGUA

C O L O M B I A

V E N E Z U E L A

SAN JOSÉ

COSTA RICA

Toucan

P A N A M A

PANAMA CITY

PANAMA CANAL

Spider monkey

0	200	400	600	800 Kilometers
0	100	200	300	400	500 Miles

13 14 15 16 17 18 19 20 21 22 23

SOUTH AMERICA

Ancient Inca city at Machu Picchu, Peru.

THE CONTINENT of South America is made up of great mountain ranges, thick forests, wide plains, and deserts. Running from north to south down the western side of South America are the snow-capped peaks of the Andes. These mountains are amongst the most recently formed on Earth and in places they are still slowly rising. Along the range of mountains are hundreds of volcanoes, some of which are still active. Many of the streams and rivers which join together to form the mighty Amazon River start in the Andes. The Amazon basin, which lies across the equator, is a hot, wet region which contains the largest tropical rain forest in the world.

The flat, fertile grasslands of the Pampas in the southeast of the continent are used for rearing cattle on huge farms called ranches, and for growing wheat. Farther south lies the colder, desert landscape of Patagonia. At the tip of the continent is Cape Horn, for centuries feared by sailors because fierce storms rage there for much of the year.

Peruvians in national costume.

In 1498 Christopher Columbus became the first European to see the coast of South America. Europeans quickly colonized the continent, and until the beginning of the 19th century South America was ruled by Spain and Portugal. Argentina was the first country to gain its independence, in 1816. The people of South America are descended from American Indians, Europeans, and Africans. Spanish is the main language, except in Brazil, where Portuguese is spoken. Many Indians speak their own languages.

About half of South America's people make their living from farming. Most farmers grow just enough beans or corn for their families to live on, but there are large plantations where coffee, sugarcane, wheat, and other crops are grown. South America is also rich in natural resources, such as oil, gold, silver, copper, iron, tin, and lead.

Saw mill on the Amazon River.

FACTS ABOUT SOUTH AMERICA

Area: 6,886,000 sq miles (17,835,000 sq km).

Population: 283,519,000.

Number of independent countries: 12.

Largest countries: Brazil, 3,286,726 sq miles (8,511,965 sq km); Argentina, 1,072,515 sq miles (2,777,815 sq km).

Most populated countries: Brazil, 144,369,000; Argentina, 31,506,000.

Largest cities: São Paulo (Brazil), 15,175,000; Buenos Aires (Argentina), 10,750,000; Rio de Janeiro (Brazil), 10,150,000.

Highest mountains: Aconcagua (Argentina), 22,834 ft (6,960 m), the world's highest extinct volcano; Ojos del Salado (Argentina-Chile), 22,664 ft (6,908 m), the world's highest active volcano; Bonete (Argentina), 22,546 ft (6,872 m).

Longest rivers: Amazon, 4,000 miles (6,437 km); Paraná, 2,796 miles (4,499 km); Madeira, 1,988 miles (3,199 km); São Francisco, 1,988 miles (3,199 km); Tocantins, 1,640 miles (2,639 km).

Main deserts: Atacama (Chile), about 31,000 sq miles (80,290 sq km); Patagonia (Argentina), about 300,000 sq miles (770,000 sq km).

Largest forest area: Amazon basin, about 2,700,000 sq miles (7,000,000 sq km).

Largest lake: Lake Titicaca (Peru-Bolivia), 3,220 sq miles (8,340 sq km). Titicaca is also the highest navigable lake in the world.

Largest island: Tierra del Fuego (Chile-Argentina), 18,140 sq miles (47,000 sq km).

World's wettest place: Tutunendo (Colombia) has an average annual rainfall of 463.4 in (11,770 mm).

World's driest place: Parts of the Atacama Desert (Chile) have an average annual rainfall of nil. In 1971 rain fell there for the first time in over 400 years.

World's highest waterfall: Angel Falls on the River Carrao (Venezuela) has a total drop of 3,212 ft (979 m).

World's largest lagoon: Lagoa dos Patos (Brazil) covers 4,110 sq miles (10,645 sq km).

A
B
C
D

NORTH AMERICA

ATLANTIC

AFRICA

GULF OF MEXICO

GREATER ANTILLES

LESSER ANTILLES

CARIBBEAN SEA

CENTRAL AMERICA

GULF OF PANAMA

LAKE MARACAIBO

Orinoco

GUIANA HIGHLANDS

MARAJO ISLAND

GALAPAGOS ISLANDS

Negro

Amazon

A M A Z O N

B A S I N

Madeira

Tocantins

Parnaíba

São Francisco

△ MT. HUASCARAN 22,204 ft

M A T O G R O S S O

B R A Z I L I A N HIGHLANDS

PACIFIC OCEAN

A N D E S

LAKE TITICACA

LAKE POOPO

GRAN CHACO

Paraguay

Paraná

TRINIDADE

ATACAMA DESERT

OJOS DEL SALADO 22,664 ft
△ BONETE 22,546 ft

Paraná

Uruguay

LAGOA DOS PATOS

△ MT. ACONCAGUA 22,834 ft

P A M P A S

RÍO DE LA PLATA

TRISTAN DA CUNHA

A N D E S

PATAGONIA

BAHIA BLANCA

GULF OF ST. MATIAS

L

FALKLAND ISLANDS (ISLAS MALVINAS)

SOUTH GEORGIA ISLAND

M

TIERRA DEL FUEGO

CAPE HORN

DRAKE PASSAGE

SOUTH SHETLAND ISLANDS

SOUTH SANDWICH ISLANDS

N

O

A N T A R C T I C A

O C E A N

NORTHERN SOUTH AMERICA

THE NORTHERN PART of South America is dominated by the vast, humid Amazon rain forest and by the high, snow-capped Andes Mountains in the west. The Amazon River is the second longest in the world, after the Nile, and runs for 4,000 miles (6,437 km) from its source in the Peruvian Andes to its mouth in northern Brazil. Every hour the Amazon delivers an average of 170 billion gallons (773 billion liters) of water into the Atlantic.

The Andes region of Peru was the center of the great Inca empire, which flourished in the 15th and 16th centuries. It was destroyed in 1532-33 by the Spanish conquistadors, led by Francisco Pizarro. The Incas were brilliant engineers, building roads and canals through difficult mountain landscapes. They were also skilled scientists, craftsmen, and farmers.

Brazil is by far the largest country in South America, both in size and population. In the overcrowded cities of southeast Brazil, such as São Paulo and Rio de Janeiro, large numbers of poor people live in slums known as "favelas."

In recent years, political and social problems have caused much upheaval in this region. Some of the nations are ruled by dictators. Colombia is one of the most dangerous countries in the world because of its ruthless drug trade. Tourism, however, remains an important source of income in South America.

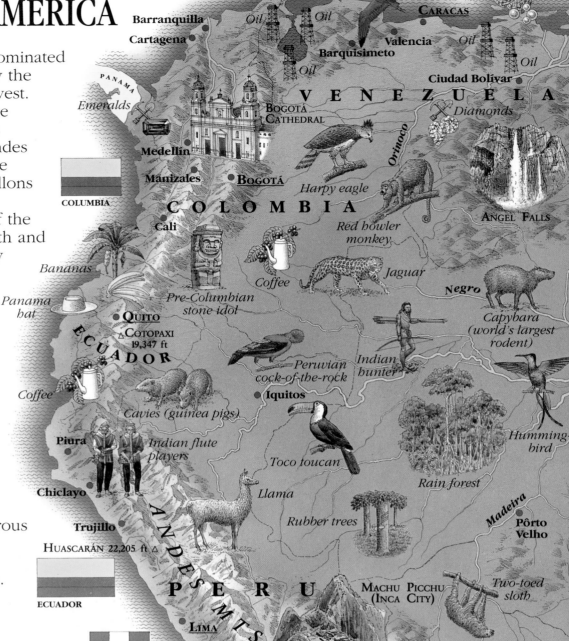

THE AMAZON RAIN FOREST

The Amazon rain forest covers an area larger than Western Europe and supports more than one-fifth of the world's plant and animal species. It is also the home of tribes of Indians who have lived there for thousands of years. But each year about 77,200 sq miles (200,000 sq km) of forest is cut down for farming and mining. As a result of the destruction of the forest, many of the plants and animals are disappearing.

GALÁPAGOS ISLANDS
(ECUADOR)

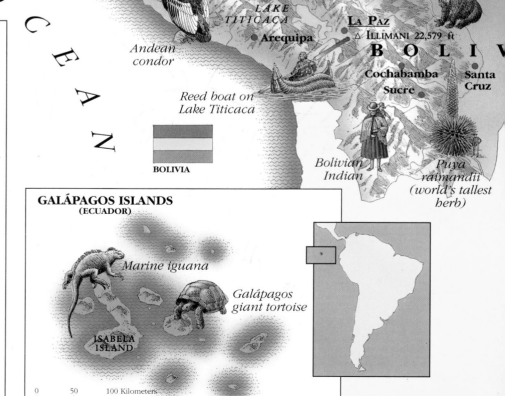

Marine iguana

Galápagos giant tortoise

ISABELA ISLAND

0   50   100 Kilometers
0   25   50   75 Miles

Map labels:

Scarlet Ibis — Pearls
Barranquilla — Oil — Oil — CARACAS
Cartagena — Valencia — Oil
Barquisimeto — Oil
PANAMA — Ciudad Bolívar
Emeralds — VENEZUELA
BOGOTÁ CATHEDRAL — Diamonds
Medellín — Orinoco
Manizales — BOGOTÁ — ANGEL FALLS
COLUMBIA — Harpy eagle
COLOMBIA
Cali — Red howler monkey
Bananas — Coffee — Jaguar — Negro
Pre-Columbian stone idol — Capybara (world's largest rodent)
Panama hat — QUITO — COTOPAXI 19,347 ft
ECUADOR — Peruvian cock-of-the-rock — Indian hunter
Coffee — Iquitos
Cavies (guinea pigs) — Hummingbird
Piura — Indian flute players — Toco toucan
Llama — Rain forest
Chiclayo — Rubber trees — Madeira
Trujillo — Pôrto Velho
HUASCARÁN 22,205 ft
ECUADOR — PERU — Machu Picchu (Inca City) — Two-toed sloth
PACIFIC — LIMA
PERU — Spectacled bear
Andean condor — LAKE TITICACA
LA PAZ — ILLIMANI 22,579 ft
Arequipa — BOLIVIA
Reed boat on Lake Titicaca — Cochabamba — Santa Cruz
Sucre
OCEAN
BOLIVIA — Bolivian Indian — Puya raimandii (world's tallest herb)

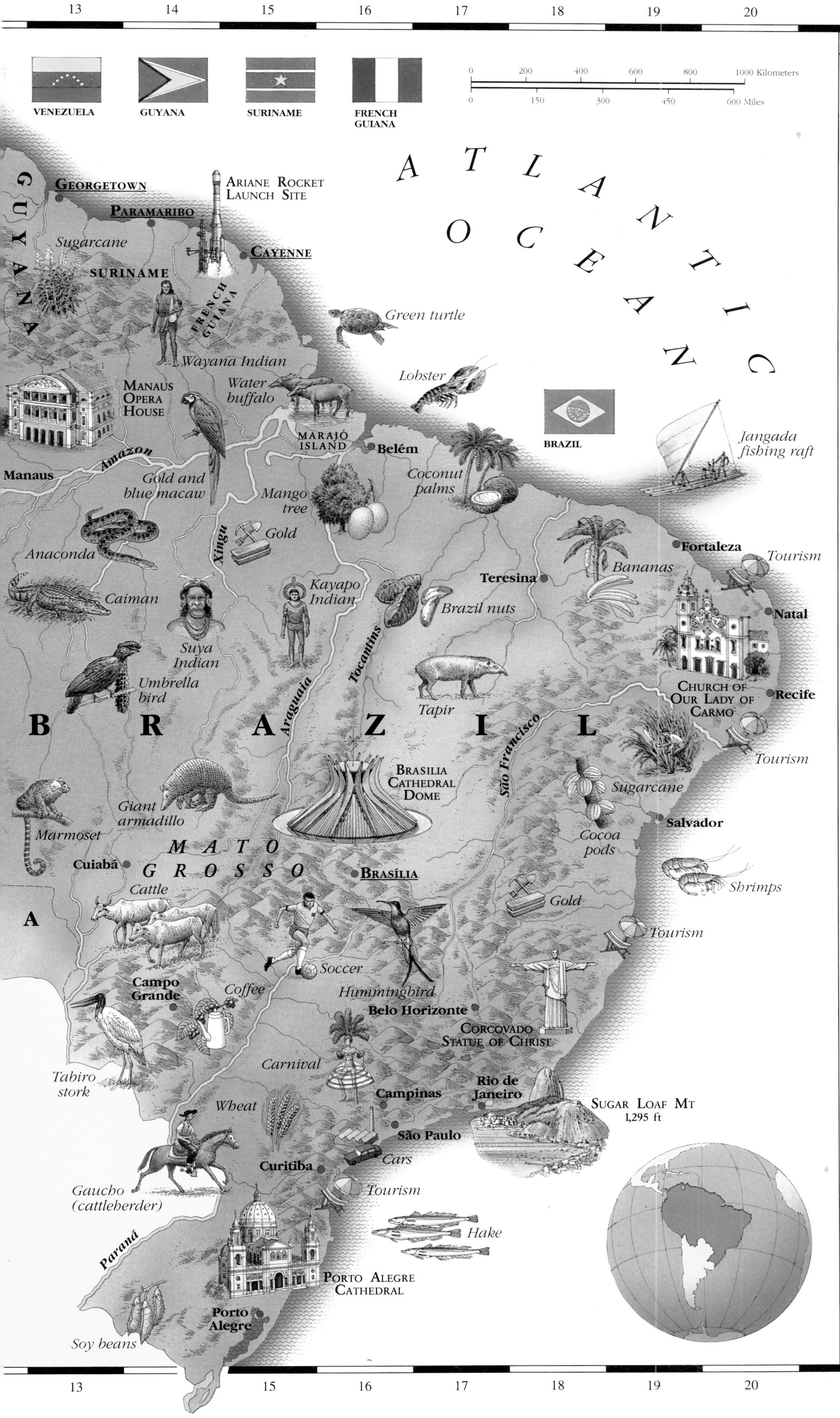

VENEZUELA

GUYANA

SURINAME

FRENCH
GUIANA

0   200   400   600   800   1000 Kilometers

0   150   300   450   600 Miles

GUYANA

GEORGETOWN

PARAMARIBO

ARIANE ROCKET
LAUNCH SITE

CAYENNE

A T L A N T I C

Sugarcane

SURINAME

Wayana Indian

Green turtle

FRENCH GUIANA

Water
buffalo

Lobster

O C E A N

MANAUS
OPERA
HOUSE

Gold and
blue macaw

MARAJÓ
ISLAND

Belém

Manaus

Amazon

BRAZIL

*Coconut
palms*

*Jangada
fishing raft*

Anaconda

Mango
tree

Gold

Xingu

Kayapo
Indian

Fortaleza

Tourism

Caiman

Suya
Indian

Brazil nuts

Teresina

Bananas

Umbrella
bird

Tocantins

Araguaia

Tapir

Natal

CHURCH OF
OUR LADY OF
CARMO

Recife

B R A Z I L

Giant
armadillo

BRASILIA
CATHEDRAL
DOME

São Francisco

Sugarcane

Tourism

Marmoset

*Cocoa
pods*

Salvador

Cuiabá

M A T O
G R O S S O

BRASÍLIA

Gold

Shrimps

A

Cattle

Soccer

Tourism

**Campo
Grande**

Coffee

Hummingbird

Belo Horizonte

CORCOVADO
STATUE OF CHRIST

*Tabiro
stork*

Carnival

Campinas

**Rio de
Janeiro**

Wheat

SUGAR LOAF MT
1,295 ft

São Paulo

Curitiba

Cars

Tourism

Paraná

*Gaucho
(cattleherder)*

Hake

PORTO ALEGRE
CATHEDRAL

**Porto
Alegre**

Soy beans

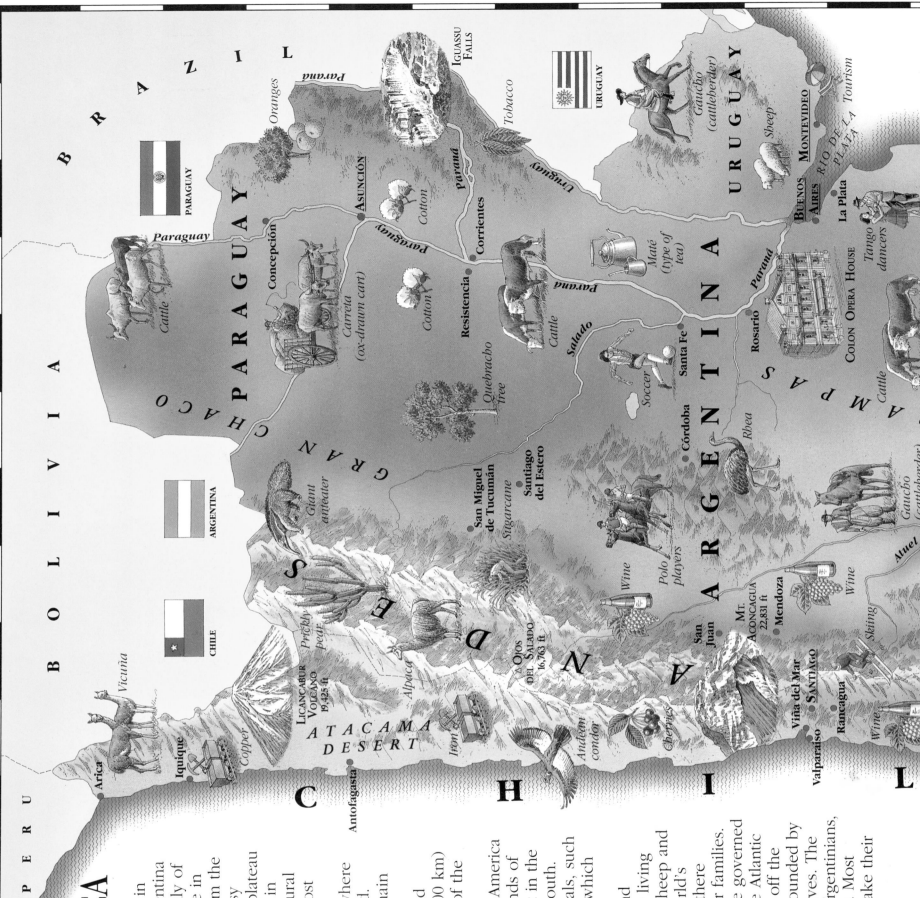

SOUTHERN SOUTH AMERICA

THE TWO LARGEST COUNTRIES in southern South America are Argentina and Chile. Their people are mainly of European descent. The landscape in Argentina varies dramatically, from the Andes mountains to forests, grassy plains and the bare, windswept plateau of Patagonia. The country is rich in mineral deposits, such as oil, natural gas, coal, and iron ore, but its most important natural resource is the Pampas – a fertile, grassy plain where large numbers of cattle are reared. Argentina is one of the world's main exporters of beef.

Chile is a long, thin strip of land stretching about 2,610 miles (4,200 km) from Peru to Punta Arenas, one of the southernmost cities in the world. Separated from the rest of South America by the Andes, Chile has many kinds of climate, from the Atacama Desert in the north, to ice and glaciers in the south. Chile has huge deposits of minerals, such as copper, iron ore and nitrates, which account for much of its wealth.

In the countries of Paraguay and Uruguay most people make their living from farming, especially raising sheep and cattle. Paraguay is among the world's poorer countries – most farmers there grow just enough to support their families.

The Falkland Islands, which are governed by the United Kingdom, lie in the Atlantic Ocean about 310 miles (500 km) off the coast of Argentina. They are surrounded by rich fishing grounds and oil reserves. The islands are also claimed by the Argentinians, who call them the *Islas Malvinas*. Most people in the Falkland Islands make their living from sheep farming.

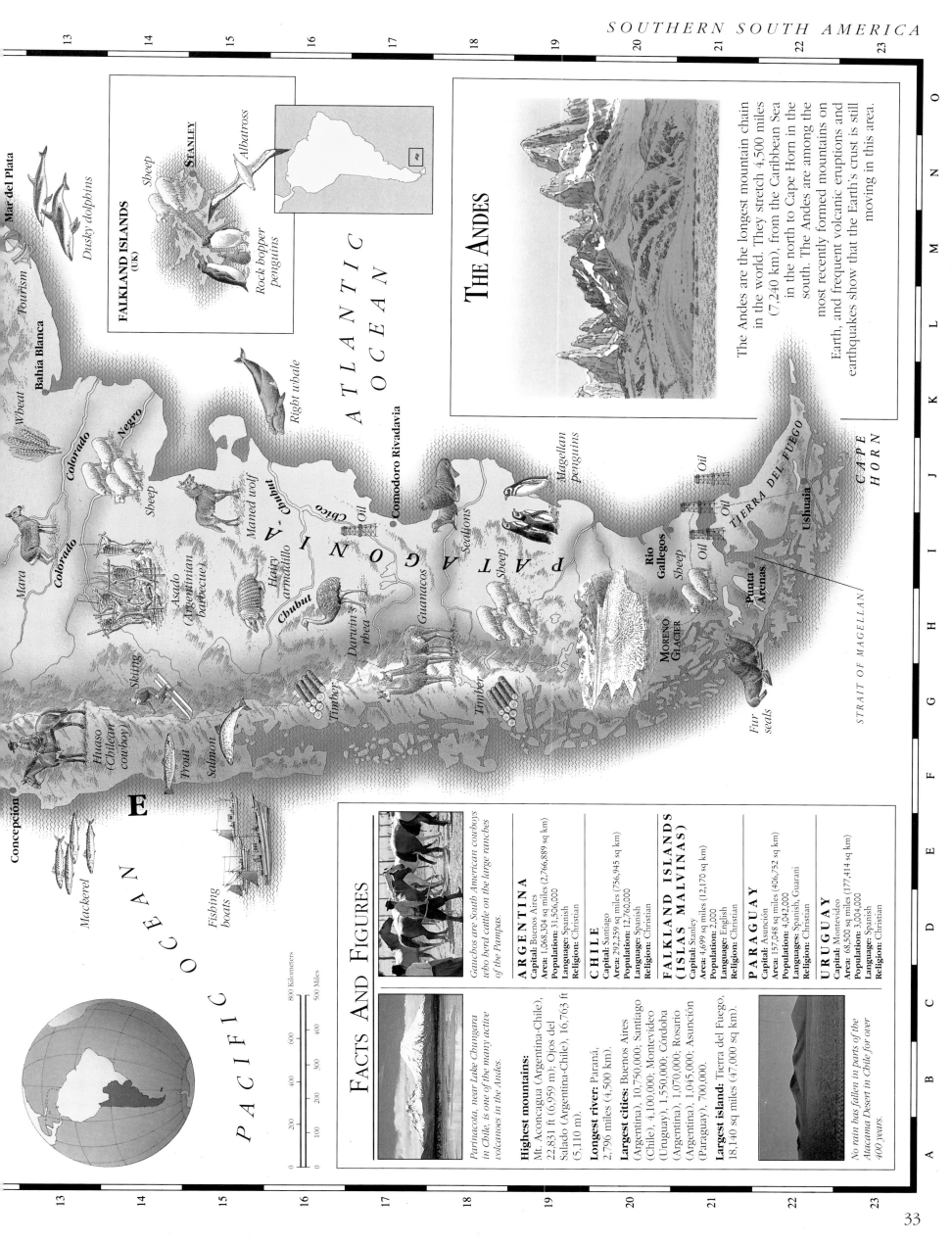

THE ANDES

The Andes are the longest mountain chain in the world. They stretch 4,500 miles (7,240 km), from the Caribbean Sea in the north to Cape Horn in the south. The Andes are among the most recently formed mountains on Earth, and frequent volcanic eruptions and earthquakes show that the Earth's crust is still moving in this area.

FALKLAND ISLANDS
(UK)

Sheep
STANLEY
Albatross
Rock hopper penguins

Mar del Plata
Tourism
Dusky dolphins
Bahia Blanca
Wheat
Colorado
Negro
Colorado
Sheep
Mara
Colorado
Asado (Argentinian barbecue)
Hairy armadillo
Maned wolf
Chubut
Chubut
Chico
Oil
Comodoro Rivadavia
Right whale

A T L A N T I C O C E A N

Darwin's rhea
Guanacos
Timber
Sheep
Sealions
Magellan penguins
Oil
Oil
Rio Gallegos
Sheep
Oil
Punta Arenas
TIERRA DEL FUEGO
Ushuaia
CAPE HORN

P A T A G O N I A

MORENO GLACIER
Timber
Fur seals

STRAIT OF MAGELLAN

Concepción
E
Huaso (Chilean cowboy)
Skiing
Trout
Salmon
Mackerel
Fishing boats

P A C I F I C O C E A N

800 Kilometers
500 Miles

0 100 200 300 400 500 600 700 800
0 100 200 300 400 500

FACTS AND FIGURES

Gauchos are South American cowboys who herd cattle on the large ranches of the Pampas.

Highest mountains:
Mt. Aconcagua (Argentina-Chile), 22,831 ft (6,959 m); Ojos del Salado (Argentina-Chile), 16,763 ft (5,110 m).

Longest river: Paraná, 2,796 miles (4,500 km).

Largest cities: Buenos Aires (Argentina), 10,750,000; Santiago (Chile), 4,100,000; Montevideo (Uruguay), 1,550,000; Córdoba (Argentina), 1,070,000; Rosario (Argentina), 1,045,000; Asunción (Paraguay), 700,000.

Largest island: Tierra del Fuego, 18,140 sq miles (47,000 sq km).

Parinacota, near Lake Chungara in Chile, is one of the many active volcanoes in the Andes.

ARGENTINA
Capital: Buenos Aires
Area: 1,068,304 sq miles (2,766,889 sq km)
Population: 31,506,000
Language: Spanish
Religion: Christian

CHILE
Capital: Santiago
Area: 292,259 sq miles (756,945 sq km)
Population: 12,760,000
Language: Spanish
Religion: Christian

FALKLAND ISLANDS (ISLAS MALVINAS)
Capital: Stanley
Area: 4,699 sq miles (12,170 sq km)
Population: 2,000
Language: English
Religion: Christian

PARAGUAY
Capital: Asunción
Area: 157,048 sq miles (406,752 sq km)
Population: 4,042,000
Languages: Spanish, Guarani
Religion: Christian

URUGUAY
Capital: Montevideo
Area: 68,500 sq miles (177,414 sq km)
Population: 3,004,000
Language: Spanish
Religion: Christian

No rain has fallen in parts of the Atacama Desert in Chile for over 400 years.

EUROPE

The headquarters of the EC in Brussels, Belgium.

EUROPE IS THE SECOND smallest continent in terms of area, but it has the second largest population of all the continents. Europe is bounded by the Atlantic and Arctic Oceans in the north and west, and in the south by the Mediterranean Sea. Europe's only land frontier – with Asia – is marked by the Ural Mountains in the USSR.

The landscape of Europe is greatly varied. In southern Europe, much of the land is hilly or mountainous. The history of this region has been greatly influenced by the Mediterranean Sea, which for centuries has been a vital trade route between Europe, Africa, and Asia.

The northern and southern parts of mainland Europe are divided by the Alps, the highest range of mountains in western Europe. The landscape of northern Europe is generally flat and is dominated by the North European Plain, which stretches from the Atlantic coast right across to the Ural Mountains. In the far north of the continent lie the mainly mountainous countries of Scandinavia.

After the end of the Second World War in 1945, the European countries were divided into two groups – the West and the East. The border between the West and the East was called the Iron Curtain, because few people were allowed to cross it.

The Eastern European countries are Romania, Poland, Yugoslavia, Czechoslovakia, Hungary, Bulgaria, Albania, and the area that was formerly East Germany. Until the late 1980s, these countries had communist governments, and many of them were closely linked to the USSR. But in recent years, some of the Eastern European countries have broken away from communist control and relations between the East and the West have improved dramatically.

The Western European countries differ in many ways, but they have in common that their governments are chosen by the people in free elections. The Western European nations are among the richest countries in the world.

Twelve countries in Western Europe have joined together to form the European Community (EC), sometimes called the Common Market. The member states are Belgium, Denmark, France, Germany, Greece, Ireland, Italy, Luxembourg, the Netherlands, Portugal, Spain, and the UK. The aim of the EC is to unite the economic resources of its members into a single economy. In the future, there may also be a form of political union between the EC countries.

In the 18th and 19th centuries, Western European countries became the first nations in the world to go through an industrial revolution. Instead of getting most of their wealth from farming, they changed to manufacturing and exporting industrial goods. Although today Europe still has the greatest concentration of industry of all the continents, a large number of Europeans still make their living from farming.

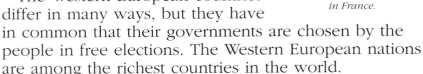

Lavender fields in France.

Vegetable market in Montenegro, Yugoslavia.

FACTS ABOUT EUROPE

Area: 4,053,309 sq miles (10,498,000 sq km). This is seven percent of the world's total land area.

Population: 690,000,000 (including the European part of the USSR). This is nearly 14 percent of the world's total population.

Number of countries: 33 (this includes 3 percent of Turkey and 25 percent of the USSR).

Largest countries: USSR – the European part of the USSR covers 2,151,000 sq miles (5,571,000 sq km), this is only 25 percent of the total area of the USSR; France, 212,936 sq miles (551,500 sq km).

Most populated countries: USSR – 188,912,000 people live in the European part of the USSR; Germany, 77,714,000.

Largest cities: Moscow (USSR), 13,100,000; London (UK), 11,100,000; Paris (France), 9,775,000; Leningrad (USSR), 5,825,000; Berlin (Germany), 3,825,000.

Highest mountains: Elbrus (USSR), 18,510 ft (5,642 m); Mont Blanc (France-Italy), 15,770 ft (4,807 m); Monte Rosa (Italy-Switzerland), 15,203 ft (4,634 m).

Longest rivers: Volga, 2,194 miles (3,531 km); Danube, 1,776 miles (2,858 km); Dnieper, 1,368 miles (2,201 km).

NORTH AMERICA

ARCTIC
OCEAN

GREENLAND

ZEMLYA
FRANTSA-IOSIFA

SVALBARD

NOVAYA
ZEMLYA

BARENTS
SEA

ASIA

NORWEGIAN
SEA

ICELAND

KJOLEN MTS

URAL MTS

LAKE
ONEGA

LAKE
LADOGA

FAEROE
ISLANDS

BRITISH
ISLES

NORTH
SEA

BALTIC SEA

CENTRAL
RUSSIAN
UPLANDS

Elbe

NORTH EUROPEAN PLAIN

Rhine

AZORES

BAY OF
BISCAY

CARPATHIANS

Dnieper

Volga

Don

Rhône

ALPS

Po

CAUCASUS

CASPIAN
SEA

Tagus

PYRENEES

HUNGARIAN
PLAIN

APENNINES

MADEIRA

CORSICA

Danube

BLACK SEA

CANARY
ISLANDS

BALEARIC
ISLANDS

SARDINIA

SICILY

MEDITERRANEAN

CRETE

CYPRUS

SEA

AFRICA

ARABIAN
PENINSULA

RED
SEA

OCEAN

INDIAN OCEAN

THE BRITISH ISLES

THE BRITISH ISLES lie off the northwestern coast of mainland Europe. They consist of two large islands – Great Britain and Ireland – surrounded by many smaller ones. The British Isles are divided into two countries: the United Kingdom and Ireland. The United Kingdom, which is often known as Britain, is itself made up of England, Wales, Scotland, and Northern Ireland.

During the 18th and 19th centuries, the United Kingdom was the first country in the world to undergo an industrial revolution. It became the world's leading manufacturing and trading nation. During this period, Britain acquired an enormous empire, covering more than a quarter of the world. Britain's colonies included Canada, Australia, New Zealand, India, and much of Africa. During the 20th century, almost all of these colonies have become independent, although they remain linked with Britain through the Commonwealth, which has 50 member countries. Today, the United Kingdom is a member of the European Community.

Until this century, Ireland was part of the United Kingdom. In 1921 the southern part of Ireland became an independent country. Most people in the south are Roman Catholic. The northern part of Ireland, where the people are mainly Protestant, remained part of the United Kingdom. The division of Ireland has caused the violent clashes which have taken place in Northern Ireland in recent years.

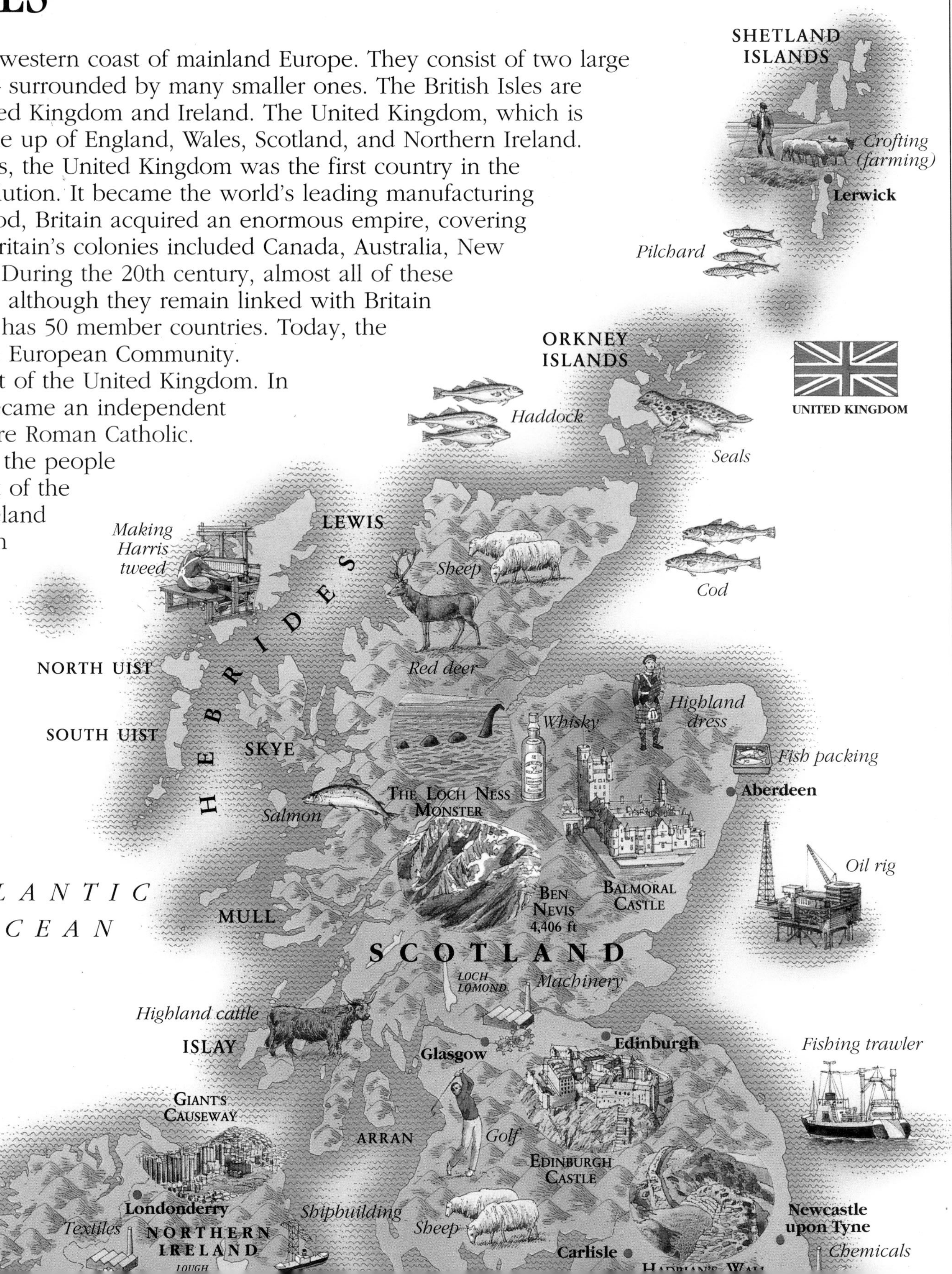
SHETLAND ISLANDS
Crofting (farming)
Lerwick
Pilchard
ORKNEY ISLANDS
UNITED KINGDOM
Haddock
Seals
Cod
LEWIS
Making Harris tweed
Sheep
HEBRIDES
Red deer
NORTH UIST
SOUTH UIST
SKYE
Whisky
Highland dress
Fish packing
Aberdeen
THE LOCH NESS MONSTER
Salmon
Oil rig
ATLANTIC OCEAN
MULL
BEN NEVIS 4,406 ft
BALMORAL CASTLE
SCOTLAND
LOCH LOMOND
Machinery
Highland cattle
ISLAY
Glasgow
Edinburgh
Fishing trawler
GIANT'S CAUSEWAY
ARRAN
Golf
EDINBURGH CASTLE
Londonderry
Textiles
NORTHERN IRELAND
Shipbuilding
Sheep
Carlisle
Newcastle upon Tyne
Chemicals

FACTS AND FIGURES

Much of Ireland's wealth comes from farming, particularly raising cattle and sheep.

Largest cities: Dublin, 1,140,000; Cork, 173,694; Limerick, 76,557.

Highest mountain: Carrauntoohil, 3,415 ft (1,038 m).

Longest river: Shannon, 240 miles (386 km).

IRELAND
Capital: Dublin
Area: 27,136 sq miles (70,284 sq km)
Population: 3,574,000
Languages: English, Irish
Religion: Christian
Currency: Punt (Irish pound)
Government: Republic

FACTS AND FIGURES

The mountainous area of Snowdonia, in northern Wales, is popular for hill walking and mountaineering.

Largest cities: London (England), 11,100,000; Manchester (England), 2,775,000; Birmingham (England), 2,675,000.

Highest mountains: Ben Nevis (Scotland), 4,406 ft (1,343 m); Snowdon (Wales), 3,560 ft (1,085 m).

Longest rivers: Severn (England-Wales), 220 miles (354 km); Thames (England), 215 miles (346 km).

World's longest bridge span: The Humber Bridge, in England, is 4,626 ft (1,410 m) long.

The traditional center of an English country town or village is its parish church.

UNITED KINGDOM
Capital: London
Area: 94,215 sq miles (244,017 sq km)
Population: 57,065,000
Language: English
Religion: Christian
Currency: Pound sterling
Government: Monarchy

ENGLAND
Capital: London
Area: 50,332 sq miles (130,360 sq km)
Population: 47,536,000

NORTHERN IRELAND
Capital: Belfast
Area: 5,452 sq miles (14,121 sq km)
Population: 1,578,000

SCOTLAND
Capital: Edinburgh
Area: 30,412 sq miles (78,769 sq km)
Population: 5,094,000

WALES
Capital: Cardiff
Area: 8,018 sq miles (20,767 sq km)
Population: 2,857,000

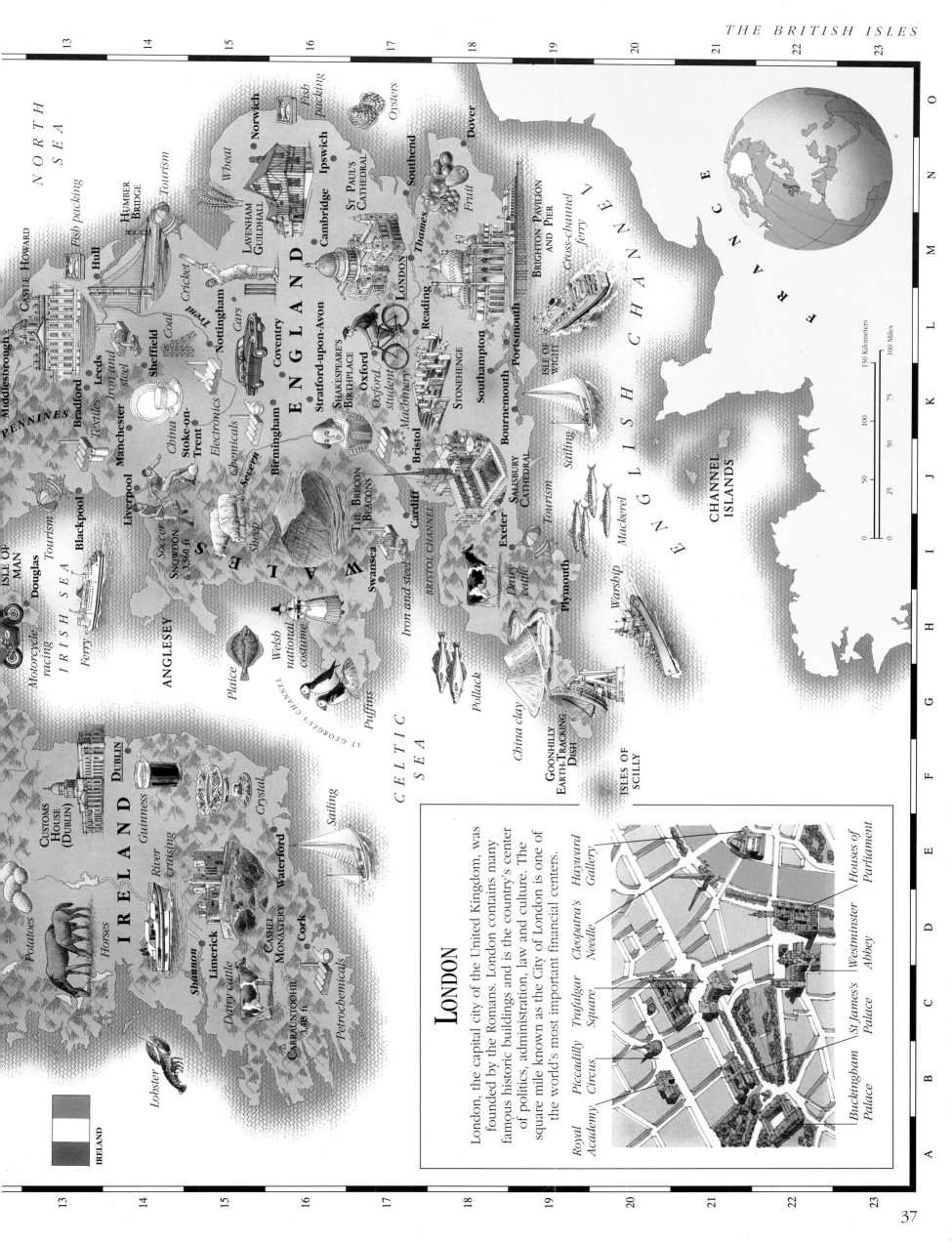

NORTH SEA

Fish packing

Castle Howard

HUMBER BRIDGE

Tourism

Middlesbrough

Hull

Wheat

Norwich

Fish packing

Oysters

LAVENHAM GUILDHALL

Ipswich

Dover

PENNINES

Bradford

Leeds

Iron and steel

Textiles

Sheffield

Coal

Trent

Cricket

Cambridge

St PAUL'S CATHEDRAL

Southend

Fruit

Thames

Manchester

China

Nottingham

Cars

ENGLAND

LONDON

Reading

BRIGHTON PAVILION AND PIER

Cross-channel ferry

Liverpool

Stoke-on-Trent

Electronics

Chemicals

Birmingham

Coventry

Stratford-upon-Avon

SHAKESPEARE'S BIRTHPLACE

Oxford

Oxford student

Machinery

STONEHENGE

Southampton

Bournemouth

Portsmouth

ISLE OF WIGHT

Blackpool

Tourism

Severn

Soccer

SNOWDON △ 3,560 ft

Sheep

THE BRECON BEACONS

Cardiff

Bristol

SALISBURY CATHEDRAL

Tourism

Sailing

ISLE OF MAN

Douglas

Motorcycle racing

IRISH SEA

Ferry

ANGLESEY

Plaice

Welsh national costume

WALES

Swansea

Iron and steel

BRISTOL CHANNEL

Exeter

Dairy cattle

Plymouth

Mackerel

Warship

CHANNEL ISLANDS

ENGLISH CHANNEL

FRANCE

Puffins

ST GEORGE'S CHANNEL

Pollack

China clay

GOONHILLY EARTH-TRACKING DISH

ISLES OF SCILLY

CELTIC SEA

CUSTOMS HOUSE (DUBLIN)

DUBLIN

Guinness

River cruising

Crystal

Waterford

Sailing

Potatoes

Horses

IRELAND

Shannon

Limerick

CASHEL MONASTERY

Cork

Dairy cattle

CARRAUNTOOHIL 3,415 ft

Petrochemicals

Lobster

IRELAND

Lobster

LONDON

London, the capital city of the United Kingdom, was founded by the Romans. London contains many famous historic buildings and is the country's center of politics, administration, law and culture. The square mile known as the City of London is one of the world's most important financial centers.

Royal Academy

Piccadilly Circus

Trafalgar Square

Cleopatra's Needle

Hayward Gallery

Houses of Parliament

Westminster Abbey

St James's Palace

Buckingham Palace

150 Kilometers

100 Miles

37

1 2 3 4 5 6 7 8 9 10 11

FRANCE

FRANCE is one of Europe's major farming and industrial nations and is famous for the food and wine it produces. The landscape in France varies dramatically from region to region and includes rich farmland; hot, dry areas; snow-capped mountains; and large forests.

France has always been an important European power. In 1789 the French over-threw their king, Louis XVI, during the French Revolution. After the revolution, Napoleon, a general in the French army, seized power and crowned himself Emperor. He went on to conquer most of mainland Europe, but was defeated at the Battle of Waterloo in 1815. During the 19th century, French explorers and soldiers won a large colonial empire in Africa and Asia.

Today France is one of the world's leading manufacturing countries, with large iron, steel, chemical, car, airplane, and textile industries. France is also rich in farming land. Its major crops include barley, oats, wheat, flax, sugarbeet, and grapes. Dairy farming is widespread and French farmers produce over 700 different types of cheese.

Tourism is another important source of wealth. There are many resorts around the coasts of France, and the Alps and Pyrenees are popular for winter sports.

UNITED KINGDOM

ENGLISH CHANNEL

ATLANTIC OCEAN

Ferry
Pollock
Shellfish
Fishing
Le Havre
Seine
Tourism
Artichokes
CHANNEL ISLANDS (UK)
MONT ST. MICHEL
BAYEUX TAPESTRY
Crab
Fishing
Dairy cattle
Tourism
Calvados (apple brandy)
BREST
QUIMPER CATHEDRAL
Breton head-dress
RENNES
Le Mans
QUIMPER
STANDING STONES (CARNAC)
TGV (high-speed train)
Tours
Warship
Loire
NANTES
CHENONCEAUX CHÂTEAU
F R
Mackerel
Eels
Wine
Beef cattle
FRANCE
Oysters
Tourism
Fishing
Brandy
Geese
Sailing
Gironde
CAVE PAINTING (LASCAUX)
Pine trees
Dordogne
Oysters
BORDEAUX
Tobacco
Pine trees
Garonne
Wine
Agen
Windsurfing
Boules (French bowls)
Walnuts
Oil
BIARRITZ
Oil
Brown bear
PAU
Ibex (type of goat)
PYRENEES
S P A I N
BAY OF BISCAY

PARIS

Visitors from all over the world flock to Paris to see its many famous sights, including the Eiffel Tower, the Arc de Triomphe, the artists' quarter of Montmartre, the tree-lined avenues, or *boulevards,* and the museums and art galleries. Paris is built on both sides of the River Seine and on two islands – the Ile St. Louis and the Ile de la Cité. On the Right Bank of the river are the capital's smart shops and fashion houses. The many cafés and bookshops on the Left Bank, or Latin Quarter, attract students and artists.

Louvre
Sacré Coeur
Arc de Triomphe
Paris Opéra
Eiffel Tower
Pompidou Center
Palais de Chaillot
Notre Dame
River Seine
Musée d'Orsay

0 50 100 150 200 Kilometers
0 25 50 75 100 125 Miles

1 2 3 4 5 6 7 8 9 10 11

13 14 15 16 17 18 19 20 21 22 23

B E L G I U M

G E R M A N Y

Dunkerque
Calais
Lille

Tourism

WORLD WAR I
MEMORIAL (ULMY)

Somme

AMIENS
CATHEDRAL

Amiens

LUXEMBOURG

Coal

Beef cattle

*Fashion
design*

CHÂTEAU BAS
(SEDAN)

Coal

Reims

Wine

Cars

PIERREFONDS
CHÂTEAU

PARIS

Champagne

Potatoes

Metz

Nancy

Strasbourg

Pigs

Storks

Wheat

Seine

*Wild
boar*

CHARTRES
CATHEDRAL

Orléans

Loire

Mulhouse

SAINTE MADELEINE
(VÉZELAY)

Mustard

CHAPEL OF NOTRE DAME
DU HAUT

Wine

Dijon

V O S G E S

CHAMBORD
CHÂTEAU

CHÂTEAUNEUF (NIEVRE)

Beaune

J U R A

S W I T Z E R L A N D

Saône

Wine

Deer

A N C E

Loire

Mâcon

Porcelain

*TGV
(high-speed train)*

Rhône

MONT BLANC
15,770 ft

Limoges

*Hunting
for truffles*

Clermont-
Ferrand

Lyon

St. Etienne

Skiing

I T A L Y

**M A S S I F
C E N T R A L**

Cycling

CHAPEL OF
ST. MICHEL
D'AIGUILHE
(LE PUY)

Grenoble

*Mountain
climbing*

Wine

*Chamois
(type of goat)*

C E V E N N E S

A L P S

Rhône

Wine

Sheep

Olives

PONT VALENTRE
(CAHORS)

Snails

*Aircraft
industry*

Montpellier

AMPHITHEATER AT ARLES

Lavender

Tourism

MONACO

Nice
Cannes

Garonne

Toulouse

WALLED TOWN
(CARCASSONNE)

Flamingos

Sailing

Fishing

Marseille
Toulon

Warship

Tourism

Tourism

MONACO

S E A

SOLAR
FURNACE
(ODEILLO)

Wine

Sardines

M E D I T E R R A N E A N

13 14 15 16 17 18 19 20 21 22 23

A
B
C
D
E
F
G
H
I
J
K
L
M
N
O

FACTS
AND FIGURES

*Amboise is one of the many historic
towns situated along the River Loire
in eastern France.*

Highest mountains:
Mont Blanc, 15,770 ft (4,807 m);
Les Ecrins, 13,461 ft (4,103 m); Pic
de Vignemale, 10,820 ft (3,298 m);
Mont Dore, 6,188 ft (1,886 m).

Longest rivers:
Loire, 625 miles (1,005 km);
Rhône-Saône, 505 miles (812 km);
Seine, 481 miles (775 km).

Largest cities:
Paris, 9,775,000; Lyon, 1,275,000;
Marseille, 1,225,000; Lille,
1,020,000; Bordeaux, 640,012.

*The TGV, which runs between Paris
and Lyon, is one of the world's fastest
trains, with a top speed of 168 mph
(270 kph).*

F R A N C E
Capital: Paris
Area: 212,936 sq miles (551,500 sq km)
Population: 55,873,000
Language: French
Religion: Christian
Currency: French franc

M O N A C O
Capital: Monaco
Area: 0.6 sq miles (1.6 sq km)
Population: 29,000
Language: French
Religion: Christian
Currency: French franc

*Sunflowers are grown all over
southern France. Their seeds are
used to make cooking oil.*

CORSICA
(FRANCE)

Bastia

C O R S I C A

Tourism

Ajaccio

Tourism

39

BELGIUM, THE NETHERLANDS, AND LUXEMBOURG

BELGIUM, THE NETHERLANDS, AND LUXEMBOURG are situated on the North European Plain, where much of the land is very flat and low lying. For this reason, they are often called the "Low Countries". The only area of higher land in the region is the hilly Ardennes forest in southern Belgium and Luxembourg.

Almost half of the Netherlands lies below sea level. There is a saying that "God made the world, but the Dutch made the Netherlands", because over the centuries the Dutch have reclaimed large areas of land from the sea. The reclaimed land, called a polder, is drained and then protected against flooding with long walls called dykes.

Belgium, the Netherlands, and Luxembourg are sometimes called "Benelux", which is a shortened version of the three country names. Although these countries are small, they have large populations. The Netherlands has one of the highest concentrations of people in Europe – an average of 936 people live in each square mile of land.

All three Benelux countries have successful industrial economies. Farming is also important, and the most up-to-date methods are used. The main products are livestock, dairy products, fruit, vegetables, and flowers. Fishing and tourism are also important sources of income. Belgium and the Netherlands have been important trading nations for many centuries. Today, Rotterdam in the Netherlands and Antwerp in Belgium are the two busiest ports in Europe.

The Benelux countries are members of the European Community, which has its headquarters in Brussels, the Belgian capital. Luxembourg is a center for European organizations, while the International Courts of Justice are situated at The Hague in the Netherlands.

THE NETHERLANDS

Gas
Windmill
Martini Tower (Groningen)
Groningen
Potatoes
Sugar beet
Hunebeds (Prehistoric Monuments)
Enschede
Hengelo
Horses
Cyclists
Cattle
Wooden clogs
Beef cattle
Zwolle
Ijssel
Leeuwarden
Ice skating
Terns
Avocet
WEST FRISIAN ISLANDS
WADDENZEE
Yachting
Bulbs
Wheat
Apeldoorn
Rhine
Arnhem
Fruit
IJSSELMEER
Canal-side houses
Traditional Dutch costume
Utrecht Cathedral Tower
Nijmegen
Maas (Meuse)
Venlo
Asparagus
Pigs
's-Hertogenbosch Cathedral
Electronics
Eindhoven
Wheat
Cheese porters
Edam cheese
Alkmaar
Haarlem
AMSTERDAM
Bulbs
Diamond cutting
Hilversum
Utrecht
Lek
Waal
Breda
Tilburg
Windmill
Antwerp Cathedral
Antwerp
Port of Antwerp
Cyclist
Leiden
Vegetables
Rotterdam
Dordrecht
Container Terminal (Rotterdam)
Schelde
Sheep
Delft pottery
THE HAGUE
Tourism
Herrings
Dam (sea barrier)
Plaice
Ferry
Ghent
Maison des Franc-Bateliers (Ghent)
Bruges Town Hall
Bruges
Ostend
Lace-making
Tourism
Shrimps

Map labels

GERMANY

FRANCE

BELGIUM

Chemicals

Maastricht

Iron and steel

Mt. Botrange 2,276 ft

Wild boar

Liège

Crystal

Louvain Town Hall

Apples

Meuse

Namur

Brussels

Chocolates

EC Headquarters

Beer

Kortrijk

Oudenaarde

Vegetables

Tournai

Tournai Cathedral

Beef cattle

Cattle

Mons

Iron and steel

Charleroi

Sambre

Pigs

Deer

ARDENNES

Walzin

THE ARDENNES FOREST

LUXEMBOURG

Clervaux

Wine

LUXEMBOURG

Esch-sur-Alzette

BELGIUM (flag)

LUXEMBOURG (flag)

AMSTERDAM

Amsterdam, the largest city in the Netherlands, is named after a dam which was built on the River Amstel in the 13th century. Like much of the country, Amsterdam lies below sea level. Large parts of the city are built on huge wooden or concrete piles sunk deep into the soggy ground. A network of canals more than 50 miles (80 km) long criss-crosses the city and helps to drain the land.

By the end of the 16th century, Amsterdam had become the leading port in the Netherlands. For the next hundred years it was also Europe's most important port and trading center and specialized in trade with the Far East. Many of the famous buildings in the city center, such as the Royal Palace and the Stock Exchange, date from this period.

Today Amsterdam is a major commercial and financial center. Many of its industries, such as processing tobacco, coffee, tea and other imported goods, diamond cutting, and shipbuilding, have developed from its historical trading connections.

The Royal Palace Nieuwe Kerk

The National Monument

Dam Square

FACTS AND FIGURES

BELGIUM
Capital: Brussels
Area: 11,781 sq miles (30,514 sq km)
Population: 9,867,000
Languages: French, Flemish, some German
Religion: Christian
Currency: Belgian franc

LUXEMBOURG
Capital: Luxembourg
Area: 998 sq miles (2,586 sq km)
Population: 371,000
Languages: Luxembourgish, French, German
Religion: Christian
Currencies: Luxembourg franc, Belgian franc

THE NETHERLANDS
National capital: Amsterdam
Seat of government: The Hague
Area: 15,770 sq miles (40,844 sq km)
Population: 14,760,000
Language: Dutch
Religion: Christian
Currency: Guilder

The historic city of Bruges in Belgium is the center of the country's lace-making industry.

Highest mountain: Mt Botrange (Belgium), 2,277 ft (694 m).

Lowest point: Prins Alexander Polder (Netherlands), 22 ft (6.7 m) below sea level.

Largest cities: Brussels (Belgium), 2,385,000; Amsterdam (Netherlands), 1,860,000; Rotterdam (Netherlands), 1,110,000; The Hague (Netherlands), 770,000.

Flower bulbs are an important export for the Netherlands. Many tourists visit the tulip fields in the spring.

Rotterdam in the Netherlands is the world's largest port. It has 76 miles (122 km) of quayside.

80 Kilometers

50 Miles

SCANDINAVIA

SCANDINAVIA consists of the four countries of Denmark, Norway, Sweden, and Finland, which are situated in northern Europe, and the island of Iceland, which lies in the North Atlantic Ocean.

The landscape of Scandinavia varies from country to country. Denmark is low lying, and much of the land is used for farming. In contrast, almost all of Norway is mountainous, and the country's coastline is dotted with long, narrow bays called fjords. Finland is a land of forests and lakes, while Sweden has an extremely varied landscape, which includes forest, farmland, mountains, and lakes. The central part of Iceland is a plateau of volcanoes, lava fields and glaciers, so most of the people live around the coast. The people of Scandinavia are the descendants of the Vikings, who lived there about 1,000 years ago. The Vikings are usually remembered as warriors and seafarers, but for most of the time they lived peacefully as farmers and fishermen.

Scandinavia has important natural resources, including the timber in its large forests, fish in the surrounding seas, iron ore in northern Sweden, and oil and natural gas in the North Sea off the coast of Norway. Today, the Scandinavian countries all have successful industrial economies, and their people enjoy a high standard of living.

THE FJORDS

During the last great Ice Age, huge ice sheets and glaciers formed over Scandinavia. The moving ice carved out deep, steep-sided valleys. When the ice sheets began to melt, about 11,000 years ago, many of these valleys were filled by the sea, forming the famous Norwegian fjords.

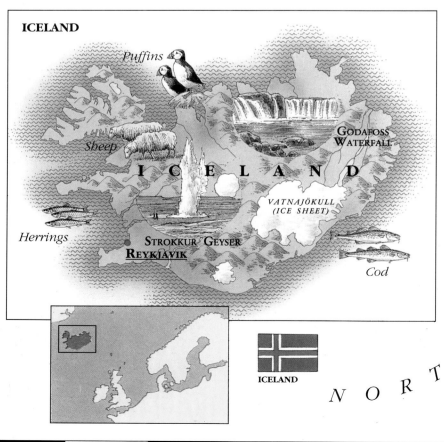

ICELAND

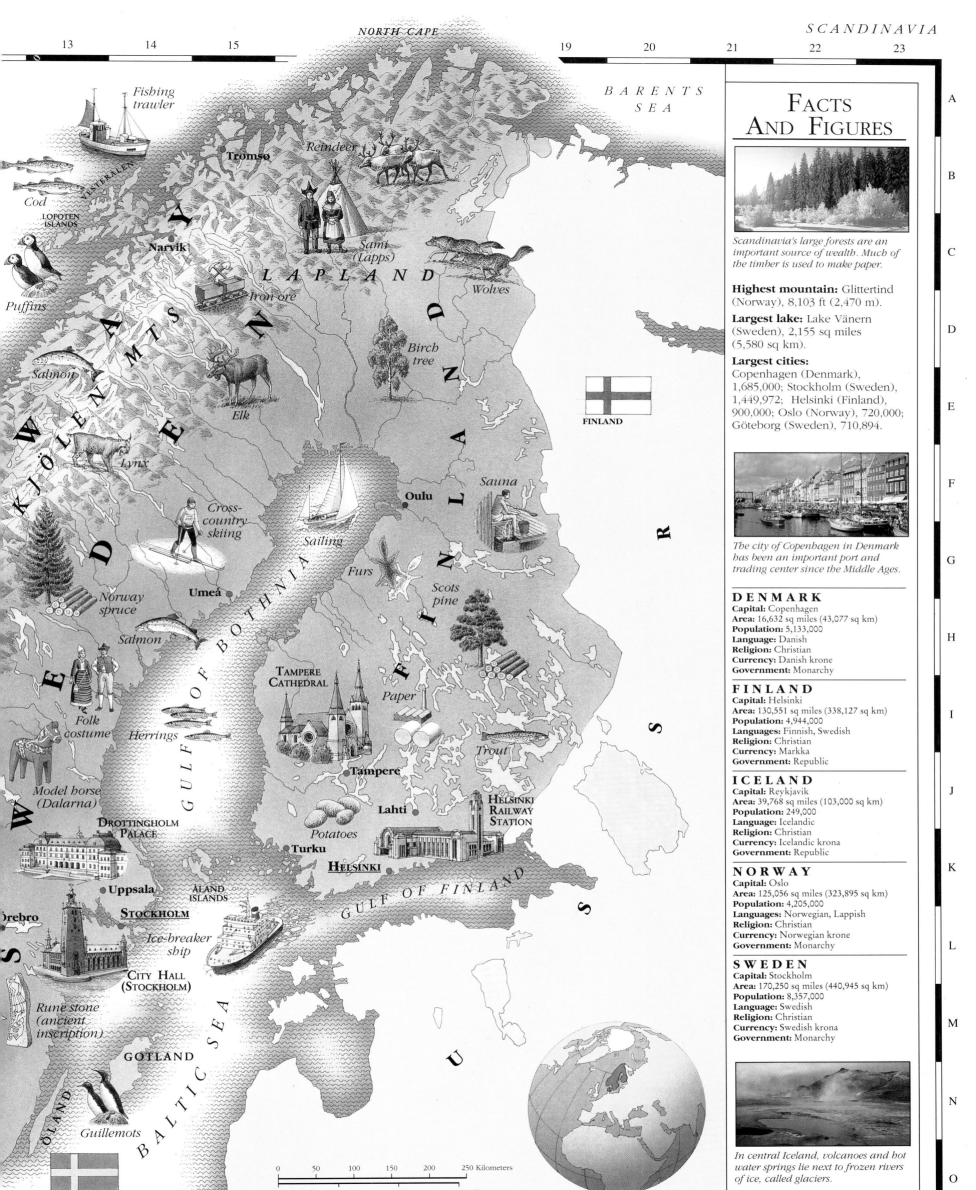

NORTH CAPE

13 14 15 19 20 21 22 23

BARENTS SEA

Fishing trawler

Cod

LOFOTEN ISLANDS

Puffins

Puffins

VESTERÅLEN

Tromsø

Reindeer

Narvik

Sami (Lapps)

Wolves

LAPLAND

Iron ore

KJØLEN MTS

Salmon

Elk

Birch tree

Lynx

Norway spruce

Cross-country skiing

Sailing

Umeå

Furs

Oulu

Sauna

Scots pine

GULF OF BOTHNIA

Folk costume

Herrings

Salmon

Paper

Model horse (Dalarna)

Dala horse

Tampere Cathedral

TAMPERE CATHEDRAL

Trout

DROTTNINGHOLM PALACE

Potatoes

Tampere

Lahti

Turku

HELSINKI RAILWAY STATION

Uppsala

ÅLAND ISLANDS

HELSINKI

Örebro

STOCKHOLM

Ice-breaker ship

GULF OF FINLAND

CITY HALL (STOCKHOLM)

Rune stone (ancient inscription)

GOTLAND

BALTIC SEA

ÖLAND

Guillemots

FINLAND

RUSSIA

SWEDEN

NORWAY

0 50 100 150 200 250 Kilometers

0 50 100 150 Miles

FACTS AND FIGURES

Scandinavia's large forests are an important source of wealth. Much of the timber is used to make paper.

Highest mountain: Glittertind (Norway), 8,103 ft (2,470 m).

Largest lake: Lake Vänern (Sweden), 2,155 sq miles (5,580 sq km).

Largest cities:
Copenhagen (Denmark), 1,685,000; Stockholm (Sweden), 1,449,972; Helsinki (Finland), 900,000; Oslo (Norway), 720,000; Göteborg (Sweden), 710,894.

The city of Copenhagen in Denmark has been an important port and trading center since the Middle Ages.

DENMARK
Capital: Copenhagen
Area: 16,632 sq miles (43,077 sq km)
Population: 5,133,000
Language: Danish
Religion: Christian
Currency: Danish krone
Government: Monarchy

FINLAND
Capital: Helsinki
Area: 130,551 sq miles (338,127 sq km)
Population: 4,944,000
Languages: Finnish, Swedish
Religion: Christian
Currency: Markka
Government: Republic

ICELAND
Capital: Reykjavik
Area: 39,768 sq miles (103,000 sq km)
Population: 249,000
Language: Icelandic
Religion: Christian
Currency: Icelandic krona
Government: Republic

NORWAY
Capital: Oslo
Area: 125,056 sq miles (323,895 sq km)
Population: 4,205,000
Languages: Norwegian, Lappish
Religion: Christian
Currency: Norwegian krone
Government: Monarchy

SWEDEN
Capital: Stockholm
Area: 170,250 sq miles (440,945 sq km)
Population: 8,357,000
Language: Swedish
Religion: Christian
Currency: Swedish krona
Government: Monarchy

In central Iceland, volcanoes and hot water springs lie next to frozen rivers of ice, called glaciers.

A B C D E F G H I J K L M N O

GERMANY, AUSTRIA, AND SWITZERLAND

THE LANDSCAPE in this region varies greatly, changing from flat plains in the north to high mountains in the south. It is crossed by two of Europe's longest rivers: the Rhine, which flows northwards to the North Sea, and the Danube, which flows eastwards to the Black Sea.

For hundreds of years, the area now called Germany consisted of many small independent states. These states were first united to form a single country in 1871. Germany rapidly became an important industrial and political power. In this century, Germany was defeated in two world wars. After World War II the country was split into two parts: the Federal Republic of Germany (West Germany) and the communist German Democratic Republic (East Germany). This split lasted for over 40 years. During this period relations between the two countries were often hostile because of their different political systems. The two German states were reunited in 1990, following the collapse of the communist government in East Germany. Today, Germany is among the world's most successful industrial nations and is the wealthiest country in Europe.

South of Germany lie the mountainous countries of Austria and Switzerland. Tourism, particularly winter sports, is an important source of wealth for both these countries. Switzerland is famous for its watches and scientific instruments, and is also a major banking and business center. The country has been neutral since 1815 and has stayed out of all the wars that have affected Europe since that time. Austria is also neutral. The tiny country of Liechtenstein, which lies between Switzerland and Austria, is only about 15 miles (24 km) long and 5 miles (8 km) wide.

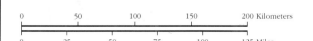

THE ALPS

EIGER 13,025 ft   MÖNCH 13,448 ft   JUNGFRAU 13,641 ft

The Alps are the longest and highest mountain range in western Europe. They stretch from southeastern France, through Italy, Switzerland, and Austria, into northern Yugoslavia – a distance of about 750 mile (1,200 km). People from around the world visit the Alps to take part in sports such as skiing and mountaineering.

BALTIC SEA

RÜGEN

Shipbuilding

Rostock

Storks

Sheep

Schwerin

Sugar beet

Dairy cattle

GERMANY

P O L A N D

Machinery   **BERLIN**

BRANDENBURG GATE

Potsdam

Magdeburg

Pigs

Elbe

Poultry
Halle

Leipzig

Textiles
Chemnitz
Zwickau

ZWINGER PALACE

Dresden

Iron and steel

Strip-mining coal

REGENSBURG CATHEDRAL

C Z E C H O S L O V A K I A

Regensburg

Beer   *Sugar beet*

Electronics

Munich
Violins

Linz

Cakes

Lipizzaner horses

VIENNA OPERA HOUSE

VIENNA

Iron and steel

Danube

Dairy cattle

A U S T R I A

HOHENSALZBURG CASTLE
Salzburg

MOZART'S BIRTHPLACE

Edelweiss

Great white pelican

MARIA-HILF-KIRCHE (GRAZ)

Graz

H U N G A R Y

Chamois (type of goat)

Skiing

Mountain climbing

Y U G O S L A V I A

I T A L Y

AUSTRIA

FACTS AND FIGURES

Belvedere Castle in Vienna was built for the Hapsburg family, who ruled Austria for many centuries.

Longest rivers: Danube, 1,776 miles (2,858 km); Rhine, 820 miles (1,320 km).

Largest lakes: Lake Geneva (Switzerland-France), 224 sq miles (580 sq km); Lake Constance (Germany-Switzerland), 208 sq miles (539 sq km).

Largest cities: Essen (Germany), 4,950,000; Berlin (Germany), 3,825,000; Hamburg (Germany), 2,225,000; Munich (Germany), 1,955,000; Vienna (Austria), 1,875,000; Frankfurt (Germany), 1,855,000; Cologne (Germany), 1,760,000; Zurich (Switzerland), 860,000.

World's tallest spire: The cathedral of Ulm in Germany has the world's tallest church spire. It is 528 ft (161 m) high.

Busiest canal: The Kiel Canal in Germany is the busiest in the world. In 1989 over 45,000 ships passed through it on their way between the North Sea and the Baltic Sea.

World's longest road tunnel: St. Gotthard tunnel in Switzerland runs under the Alps, and is 10.14 miles (16.32 km) long.

World's biggest roof: The glass roof over the Olympic Stadium in Munich measures 914,940 sq ft (85,000 sq m).

Many dairy cows graze on the slopes of the Alps. Their milk is used to make the famous Swiss chocolate.

AUSTRIA
Capital: Vienna
Area: 32,375 sq miles (83,853 sq km)
Population: 7,563,000
Language: German
Religion: Christian
Currency: Schilling
Government: Republic

GERMANY
National capital: Berlin
Seat of government: Bonn
Area: 137,804 sq miles (356,910 sq km)
Population: 77,714,000
Language: German
Religion: Christian
Currency: Deutsche Mark
Government: Republic

LIECHTENSTEIN
Capital: Vaduz
Area: 62 sq miles (160 sq km)
Population: 28,000
Language: German
Religion: Christian
Currency: Swiss franc
Government: Monarchy

SWITZERLAND
Capital: Bern
Area: 15,943 sq miles (41,293 sq km)
Population: 6,545,000
Languages: German, French, Italian
Religion: Christian
Currency: Swiss franc
Government: Republic

The city of Munich in southern Germany is famous for its annual beer festival, the Oktoberfest.

THE RHINE VALLEY

The Rhine is one of the longest rivers in Europe. It flows from Switzerland through Germany and the Netherlands to the North Sea. Boats can sail up the Rhine as far as Basel in Switzerland, and for this reason the river has been an important European trade route for many centuries. Products such as coal, iron ore and petroleum are still transported by barge along the Rhine today.

In western Germany, the Rhine flows through a spectacular, steep-sided valley dotted with ruined castles, some of which are 800 years old. In many places the sides of the valley have been terraced and are used for growing wine grapes.

One of the famous sights of the Rhine Valley is the Lorelei Rock, which is situated west of Wiesbaden. According to legend, a water nymph at the Lorelei sang to passing sailors and lured them to their deaths on the rocks.

ITALY

THE EASILY RECOGNIZABLE BOOT SHAPE OF ITALY is a thin, 500-mile (800-km) long peninsula in southern Europe, which stretches south into the Mediterranean Sea. Nearly three-quarters of the country is hilly or mountainous. In the north, the snow-covered Alps form a barrier between Italy and the rest of Europe. Running down the spine of the country are the Apennines, rugged mountains dotted with hill-top villages and small towns that have hardly changed for centuries. The Mediterranean islands of Sicily and Sardinia are also part of Italy.

Modern Italy, with Rome as its capital, only came into existence in 1870. Before then the area had been a patchwork of independent city states. These states can still be seen today in Italy's 20 "regions". Two of the states have remained independent – the Vatican City in Rome and the Republic of San Marino in northeastern Italy.

Italy has been important since Roman times, when it was the center of the greatest empire Europe had ever seen. The remains of Roman roads and buildings can still be seen all over the country and beyond. In the 14th–16th centuries, Italy was the center of an important movement in the arts, called the Renaissance. Many beautiful paintings, sculptures, buildings, and poems were produced in Italy during this period. Among Italy's most famous Renaissance writers and artists were Michelangelo, Leonardo da Vinci, Raphael, and Dante. Today millions of tourists each year visit Italy's ancient cities and art treasures.

Modern Italy is an important industrial nation, with large steel, chemical, textile, and car manufacturing industries. However, many Italians still make their living from farming. The main crops are wheat, corn, rice, grapes, and olives, and there are many fishing ports around Italy's coast.

FACTS AND FIGURES

The city of Venice is built on about 120 islands and has canals in place of streets.

Highest mountains: Mont Blanc (Italy-France), 15,771 ft (4,807 m); Monte Rosa (Italy-Switzerland), 15,203 ft (4,634 m).

Longest river: Po, 418 miles (672 km).

Largest lakes: Lake Garda, 143 sq miles (370 sq km); Lake Maggiore, 82 sq miles (212 sq km); Lake Como, 55 sq miles (145 sq km).

Largest cities: Milan, 3,750,000; Rome, 3,175,000; Naples, 2,875,000; Turin, 1,550,000.

A horse race called the Palio takes place in Siena each year. The riders wear traditional costumes dating from the 15th century.

ITALY
Capital: Rome
Area: 116,320 sq miles (301,268 sq km)
Population: 57,470,000
Language: Italian
Religion: Christian
Currency: Lira
Government: Republic

MALTA
Capital: Valletta
Area: 122 sq miles (316 sq km)
Population: 345,000
Languages: Maltese, English
Religion: Christian
Currency: Maltese pound
Government: Republic

SAN MARINO
Capital: San Marino
Area: 23 sq miles (61 sq km)
Population: 24,000
Language: Italian
Religion: Christian
Currency: Lira
Government: Republic

VATICAN CITY
Area: 0.17 sq miles (0.44 sq km)
Population: 1,000

Cars, motorcycles, tractors and trucks are among Italy's most valuable exports. Major manufacturers include Fiat, Ferrari, and Lamborghini.

(Map labels)

YUGOSLAVIA
AUSTRIA
SWITZERLAND
FRANCE
ALPS
APENNINES
LIGURIAN SEA

Chamois (type of goat)
Wine
Trieste
Udine
PINNACLES OF THE DOLOMITES
ST. MARK'S SQUARE
Venetian gondolier
Cruise liner
Sole
Ancona
ST. CHIARA (ASSISI)
Tourism
Venice
Bolzano
Trento
Padua
Ferrara
Po
Rimini
SAN MARINO
Perugia
Assisi
FLORENCE CATHEDRAL
Marmots
Skiing
LAKE GARDA
Adige
Verona
Mantua
Modena
Bologna
Ravenna
Florence
Arno
Tiber
Siena
Bergamo
Brescia
Violins
Po
Parma
Ferrari cars
LEANING TOWER OF PISA
Monte Rosa 15,203 ft
Como
Monza
Milan
MILAN CATHEDRAL
Rice
Cremona
Parmesan cheese
Marble quarry
Pisa
Tourism
Livorno
Squid
ELBA
Mont Blanc 15,771 ft
Ibex (type of goat)
Turin
Fiat cars
Genoa
Wine
La Spezia
Tourism
Tourism
Shellfish
Tourism
Ferry boat
Sardines
Olive trees

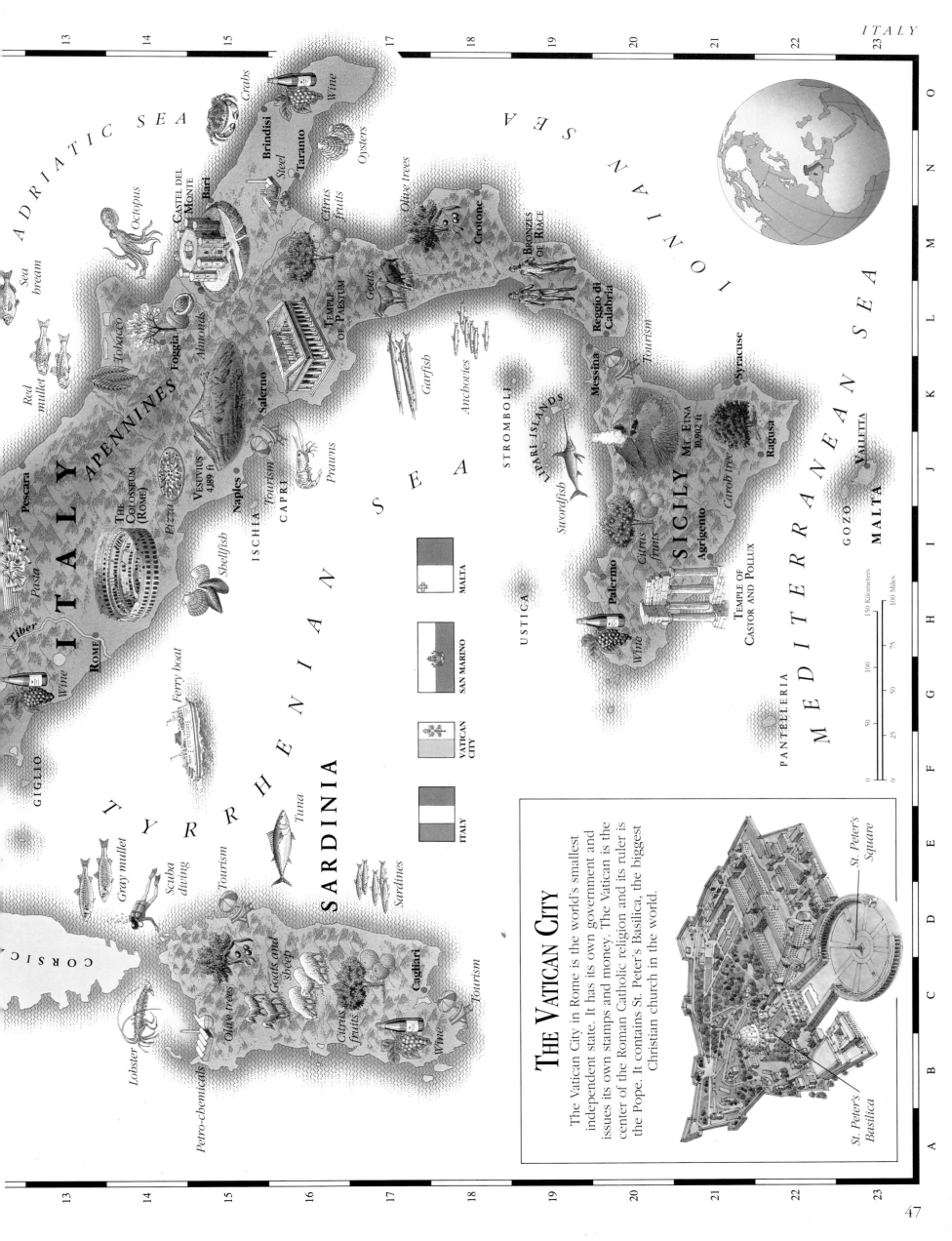

THE VATICAN CITY

The Vatican City in Rome is the world's smallest independent state. It has its own government and issues its own stamps and money. The Vatican is the center of the Roman Catholic religion and its ruler is the Pope. It contains St. Peter's Basilica, the biggest Christian church in the world.

SPAIN AND PORTUGAL

THE COUNTRIES of Spain and Portugal occupy a large, square block of land called the Iberian Peninsula in southwestern Europe. The peninsula also contains the tiny independent state of Andorra and the British colony of Gibraltar. Over the centuries, Spain and Portugal have been invaded and settled by many different peoples, including the Romans and the Moors – an Arab people from North Africa who ruled much of Spain for nearly eight centuries.

Both Spain and Portugal have a long history of exploring and trading by sea. Christopher Columbus set out from Spain when he sailed to America in 1492. In 1497 the Portuguese explorer, Vasco da Gama, became the first person to sail around Africa to India. Settlers followed the explorers, and during the 16th century Spain and Portugal came to rule vast empires in North and South America, Asia, and Africa.

Today, many people in Spain and Portugal make their living from farming or fishing. Both countries also have important manufacturing industries, producing steel, ships, cars, chemicals, and textiles. Tourism is a major source of wealth in both countries.

PORTUGAL

THE WINE TRADE

Spain and Portugal are famous for their "fortified" wines, such as sherry and port. These contain more alcohol than normal wine because brandy is added to the grape juice to fortify, or strengthen, it. This was originally done to stop the wine from going bad while it was shipped abroad. Fortified wines are left in wooden casks to mature for at least three years. Both sherry and port are named after the towns where they are produced – sherry comes from Jerez de la Frontera in southern Spain, and port from Porto in northern Portugal.

BAY OF BISCA

Shellfish
Fish packing
Iron and steel
Gijón
Apples
Santand
La Coruña
Horses
Oviedo
Coal
CAVE PAINTING (ALTAMIRA)
Santiago
CATHEDRAL OF SANTIAGO DE COMPOSTELA
Brown bear
León
Potatoes
Cattle
Vigo
Minho
Fish packing
Cockerel of Barcelos
Egyptian vulture
LEÓN CATHEDRAL
Wheat
Braga
Anchovies
Textiles
Valladolid
Porto
Douro
Cattle
S
P
Port wine
Salamanca
HOUSE OF SHELLS (SALAMANCA)
Segovia
Transporting port wine
Fish packing
Potatoes
Avila
Mackerel
Rugs
Coimbra
STATUE OF PIZARRO (TRUJILLO)
Toled
Pilchards
Tagus
PORTUGAL
TOLEDO CATHEDRAL
Olive trees
Roman Theatre
BELEM TOWER
Tagus
Wine
ROMAN TEMPLE (EVORA)
Merida
Manchego cheese
LISBON
Badajoz
Windmill
Guadiana
Sheep
Setúbal
Bulls
Fish packing
CORDOBA MOSQUE
Sardines
SEVILLE CATHEDRAL
Córdoba
Cork oak
Citrus fruits
Guadalquivir
Tourism
Pardel lynx
Seville
Holy week procession (Seville)
Tourism
Faro
Guadiana
Lobster
Sherry
Wine
Málaga
Jerez de la Frontera
ROCK OF GIBRALTAR
Cádiz
GIBRALTAR
STRAIT OF GIBRALTAR
M
Ceuta (Spain)
Tuna

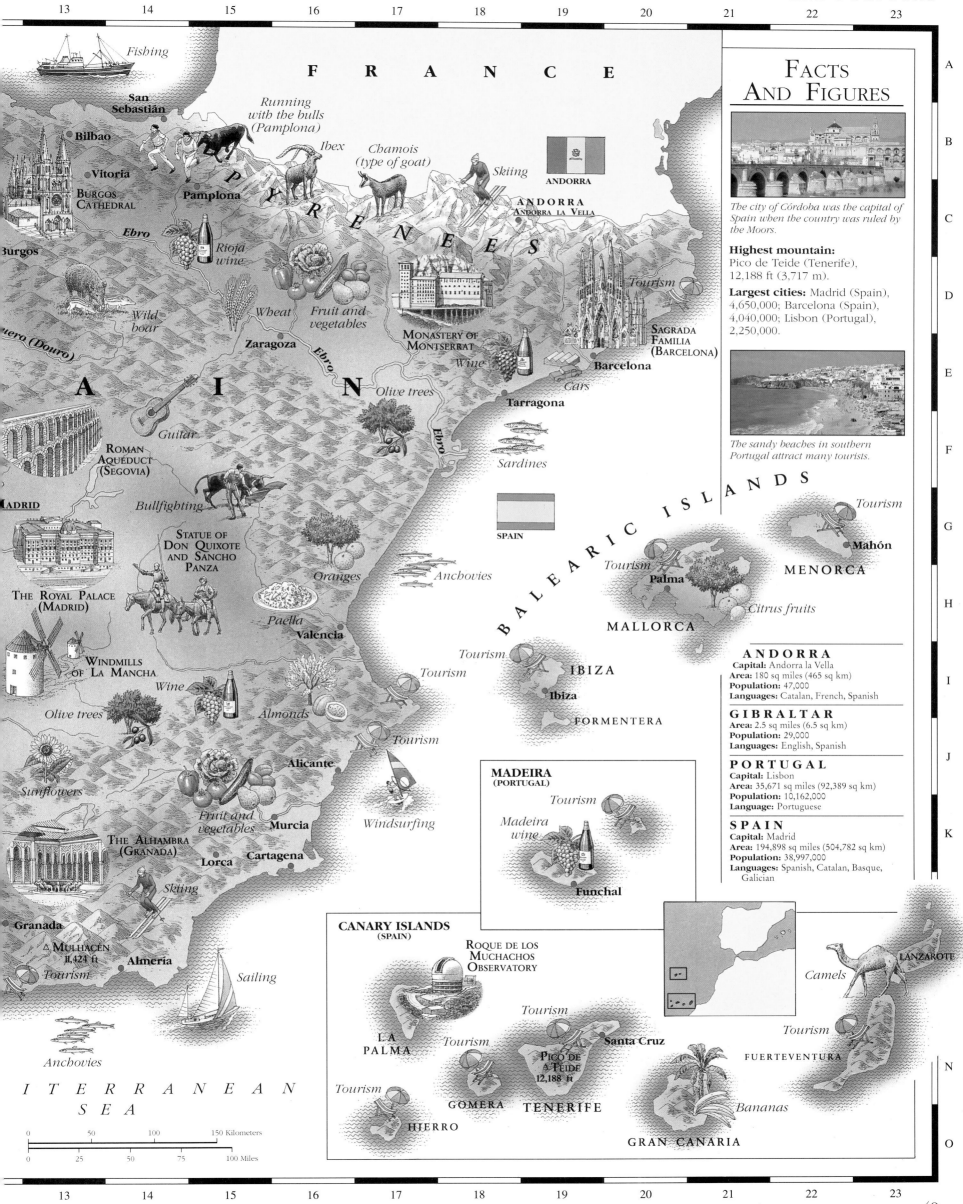

FRANCE

Fishing

San Sebastián

Bilbao

Vitoria

Running with the bulls (Pamplona)

BURGOS CATHEDRAL

Pamplona

Ibex

Chamois (type of goat)

Skiing

ANDORRA
ANDORRA LA VELLA

ANDORRA

Burgos

Ebro

Rioja wine

ero (Douro)

Wild boar

Wheat

Fruit and vegetables

ZARAGOZA

Ebro

MONASTERY OF MONTSERRAT

Wine

SAGRADA FAMILIA (BARCELONA)

Tourism

Barcelona

Tarragona

Cars

A I N

Olive trees

Guitar

Ebro

Sardines

ROMAN AQUEDUCT (SEGOVIA)

MADRID

Bullfighting

THE ROYAL PALACE (MADRID)

STATUE OF DON QUIXOTE AND SANCHO PANZA

Oranges

Anchovies

Paella

SPAIN

Tourism

B A L E A R I C   I S L A N D S

Tourism

MENORCA

Mahón

Tourism

Palma

Citrus fruits

MALLORCA

Tourism

IBIZA

WINDMILLS OF LA MANCHA

Wine

Almonds

Valencia

Tourism

Tourism

Ibiza

FORMENTERA

Olive trees

Sunflowers

Fruit and vegetables

Alicante

Tourism

THE ALHAMBRA (GRANADA)

Murcia

Windsurfing

Lorca

Cartagena

Skiing

Granada

△ **MULHACÉN** 11,424 ft

Tourism

Almería

Sailing

Anchovies

I T E R R A N E A N   S E A

CANARY ISLANDS (SPAIN)

ROQUE DE LOS MUCHACHOS OBSERVATORY

Tourism

LA PALMA

Tourism

Tourism

Santa Cruz

Tourism

PICO DE TEIDE 12,188 ft

GOMERA

TENERIFE

Tourism

HIERRO

Bananas

GRAN CANARIA

MADEIRA (PORTUGAL)

Tourism

Madeira wine

Funchal

Camels

LANZAROTE

Tourism

FUERTEVENTURA

0   50   100   150 Kilometers
0   25   50   75   100 Miles

FACTS AND FIGURES

The city of Córdoba was the capital of Spain when the country was ruled by the Moors.

Highest mountain:
Pico de Teide (Tenerife), 12,188 ft (3,717 m).

Largest cities: Madrid (Spain), 4,650,000; Barcelona (Spain), 4,040,000; Lisbon (Portugal), 2,250,000.

The sandy beaches in southern Portugal attract many tourists.

ANDORRA
Capital: Andorra la Vella
Area: 180 sq miles (465 sq km)
Population: 47,000
Languages: Catalan, French, Spanish

GIBRALTAR
Area: 2.5 sq miles (6.5 sq km)
Population: 29,000
Languages: English, Spanish

PORTUGAL
Capital: Lisbon
Area: 35,671 sq miles (92,389 sq km)
Population: 10,162,000
Language: Portuguese

SPAIN
Capital: Madrid
Area: 194,898 sq miles (504,782 sq km)
Population: 38,997,000
Languages: Spanish, Catalan, Basque, Galician

CENTRAL AND EASTERN EUROPE

THIS REGION has always been one of the most unstable parts of Europe, and the boundaries between the countries have changed many times. After World War II, all the countries in this region, apart from Greece, became part of the "Eastern Bloc". They had communist governments and strong links with the USSR. In recent years there have been important political changes in the region. Many of the countries are now establishing demo-cratic forms of government and are building closer links with their neighbors in Western Europe.

The northern part of this region is dominated by Poland. The country of Poland has been much fought over, and for long periods it did not exist as

a separate nation. Poland is rich in coal and copper, and has large textile, iron, steel, and shipbuilding industries. Farming is also important: the main crops are potatoes, wheat, and sugar beets. Czechoslovakia was only created as an independent country in 1918. The country is made up of two separate peoples, the Czechs and the Slovaks, each speaking a different language. Many Czechoslovaks are farmers, but the country also has important coal, iron, and steel industries.

To the south lies the area known as the Balkans, which includes the countries of Greece, Albania, Yugoslavia, Bulgaria, Romania and Hungary. The present pattern of countries in the Balkans was only formed during the rearrangement of European borders at the end of the two world wars.

Yugoslavia has a large tourist industry with popular beaches along its Adriatic coast. Greece, too, is one of the most popular holiday destinations in Europe and visitors go there to explore its many islands and ancient buildings.

FACTS AND FIGURES

Every year many tourists visit the picturesque old towns along Yugoslavia's Adriatic coast.

Largest cities: Athens (Greece), 3,027,331; Budapest (Hungary), 2,565,000.

Longest river: Danube, 1,776 miles (2,858 km).

Highest mountains: Musala (Bulgaria), 9,596 ft (2,925 m); Mt Olympus (Greece), 9,570 ft (2,917 m).

Warsaw, in Poland, was badly damaged during World War II, but many old buildings have been rebuilt.

POLAND

HUNGARY

BULGARIA

ROMANIA

CZECHOSLOVAKIA

400 Kilometers
250 Miles
300
200
150
100
100
50

BALTIC SEA

Shipbuilding
Shipbuilding
Tourism
Gdansk
Chemicals
Potatoes
Bydgoszcz
Poznan
Szczecin
Wooden windmills
Oder
Copper
Folk costume
PRAGUE
CATHEDRAL OF ST VITUS
Pilsen lager
Skoda cars
Brno
Bratislava
BRATISLAVA CASTLE
Wine
BUDAPEST
Debrecen
Wild

POLAND
Vistula
WARSAW
Lodz
Wroclaw
Walbrzych
Coal
Iron and steel
Katowice
Krakow
Ostrava
Coal

SWIETA LIPKA BASILICA
European bison
MASURIAN LAKES
Pigs
POZNAN TOWN HALL

Bug
PALACE OF CULTURE
Lublin
Wheat
Vistula
Sheep
Sugar beet
Kosice
CARPATHIAN MTS
Skiing
Morava
Chemicals
PARLIAMENT BUILDING (BUDAPEST)

C Z E C H O S L O V A K I A

H U N G A R Y

A U S T R I A

G E R M A N Y

R U S S I A

Spruce
Cattle
Machinery
Skiing

ALBANIA
Capital: Tirana
Area: 11,099 sq miles (28,748 sq km)
Population: 3,145,000
Language: Albanian
Religions: Moslem, Christian
Currency: Lek
Government: Communist republic

BULGARIA
Capital: Sofia
Area: 42,823 sq miles (110,912 sq km)
Population: 8,995,000
Language: Bulgarian
Religions: Christian, Moslem
Currency: Lev
Government: Republic

CZECHOSLOVAKIA
Capital: Prague
Area: 49,373 sq miles (127,876 sq km)
Population: 15,610,000
Languages: Czech, Slovak
Religions: Christian
Currency: Koruna
Government: Republic

GREECE
Capital: Athens
Area: 50,961 sq miles (131,990 sq km)
Population: 10,030,000
Language: Greek
Religion: Christian
Currency: Drachma
Government: Republic

HUNGARY
Capital: Budapest
Area: 35,919 sq miles (93,032 sq km)
Population: 10,604,000
Language: Hungarian
Religion: Christian
Currency: Forint
Government: Republic

POLAND
Capital: Warsaw
Area: 120,728 sq miles (312,685 sq km)
Population: 37,873,000
Language: Polish
Religion: Christian
Currency: Zloty
Government: Republic

ROMANIA
Capital: Bucharest
Area: 91,699 sq miles (237,500 sq km)
Population: 23,052,000
Languages: Romanian
Religion: Christian
Currency: Leu
Government: Republic

YUGOSLAVIA
Capital: Belgrade
Area: 98,766 sq miles (255,804 sq km)
Population: 23,552,000
Languages: Serbo-Croat, Albanian, Macedonian, Slovene
Religion: Christian
Currency: Dinar
Government: Republic

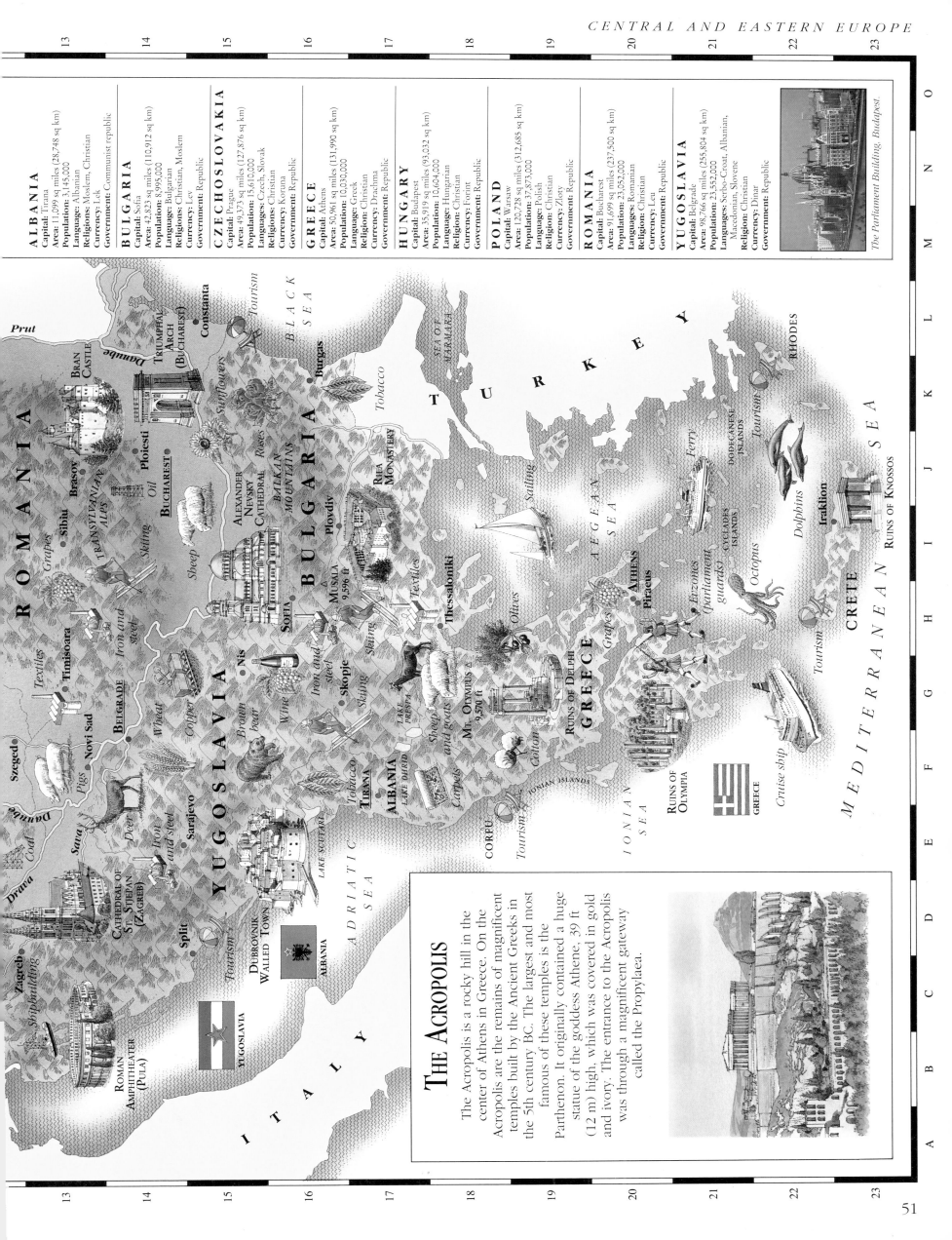

The Parliament Building, Budapest.

THE ACROPOLIS

The Acropolis is a rocky hill in the center of Athens in Greece. On the Acropolis are the remains of magnificent temples built by the Ancient Greeks in the 5th century BC. The largest and most famous of these temples is the Parthenon. It originally contained a huge statue of the goddess Athene, 39 ft (12 m) high, which was covered in gold and ivory. The entrance to the Acropolis was through a magnificent gateway called the Propylaea.

ASIA

Guilin, China.

ASIA is the largest continent in the world, occupying nearly a third of the world's total land area. It contains the world's highest point (Mount Everest), as well as its lowest (the Dead Sea). Asia also has the largest population of any continent – six out of every ten people in the world live there. All the world's major religions – including Judaism, Islam, Buddhism, Christianity, Confucianism, and Hinduism – originated in Asia.

In a continent of this size, stretching from the Arctic to the equator, there are great contrasts. The climate ranges from some of the coldest places on earth to some of the hottest, and from some of the driest places to some of the wettest. Asia contains the world's largest country (the USSR) and some of its smallest countries. In parts of Asia there are huge concentrations of people, yet there are also vast regions which are almost uninhabited.

Siberia, the Asian part of the USSR, is mainly covered by coniferous forest. It is bitterly cold in winter, and few people live there. Bordering the USSR in the east is China. Most of China's one billion people live in the eastern part of the country where the land is good for farming.

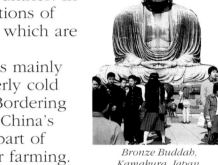
Bronze Buddah, Kamakura, Japan.

The population of the Gobi desert and the high Plateau of Tibet is very small. South of the Himalayas, the world's highest mountain range, lies Southern Asia, which is often called the Indian subcontinent. Around one billion people live there, mainly along the fertile coasts and on the plains of the Ganges and Indus rivers in the north.

Southwestern Asia is also known as the Middle East. The world's earliest known civilizations grew up here in the area called the Fertile Crescent, which extends from the Mediterranean Sea across Syria to the land between the Tigris and Euphrates rivers. Among the ancient peoples of the Fertile Crescent were the Sumerians, Assyrians, Babylonians, and Hebrews. This area contrasts sharply with the almost empty deserts of the Arabian Peninsula, flanked by the oil-rich nations of the Persian Gulf, such as Saudi Arabia, Qatar, and Bahrain.

Southeastern Asia is situated along the equator. Much of the region is made up of thousands of islands, large and small. These include the countries of Indonesia, Malaysia, and the Philippines.

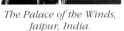
The Palace of the Winds, Jaipur, India.

FACTS ABOUT ASIA

Area: 16,838,365 sq miles (43,608,000 sq km).

Population: 3,074,000,000.

Number of independent countries: 42 (this includes 6 percent of Egypt, 97 percent of Turkey, and 75 percent of the USSR).

Largest countries: The Asian part of the USSR, 6,498,500 sq miles (16,831,000 sq km) – this is only 75 percent of the total area of the USSR; China, 3,705,691 sq miles (9,597,000 sq km).

Most populated countries: China, 1,083,889,000 (the largest population in the world); India, 813,990,000.

Largest cities: Tokyo (Japan), 27,700,000; Seoul (South Korea), 15,850,000; Shanghai (China), 9,300,000.

Highest mountains: Mt. Everest (Nepal-China), the highest in the world, 29,028 ft (8,848 m); K2 (Qogir Feng) (Pakistan-China), 28,250 ft (8,611 m).

Longest rivers: Chang Jiang (Yangtze), 3,915 miles (6,300 km); Huang He (Yellow River), 3,395 miles (5,463 km); Ob-Irtysh, 3,362 miles (5,410 km); Amur, 2,761 miles (4,443 km).

Main deserts: Gobi (Mongolia-China), about 500,000 sq miles (1,295,000 sq km); Thar (Pakistan-India), about 74,000 sq miles (192,000 sq km).

Largest lakes: Caspian Sea (USSR-Iran), the largest in the world, 143,205 sq miles (371,000 sq km); Aral Sea (USSR), 25,285 sq miles (65,500 sq km).

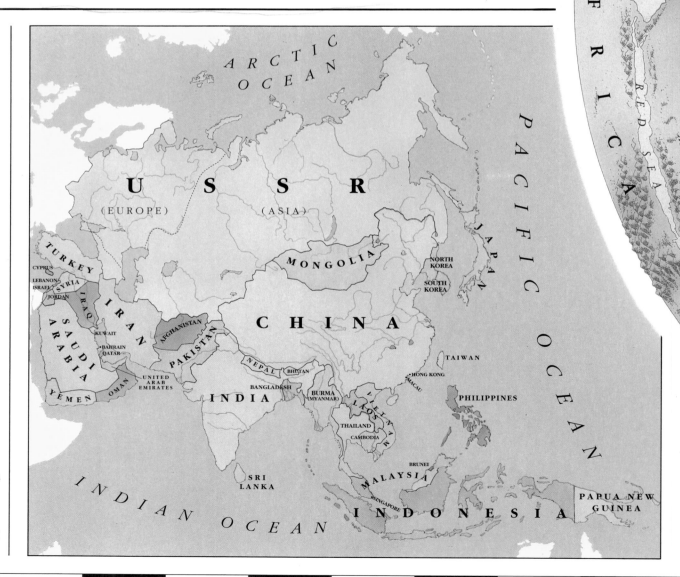

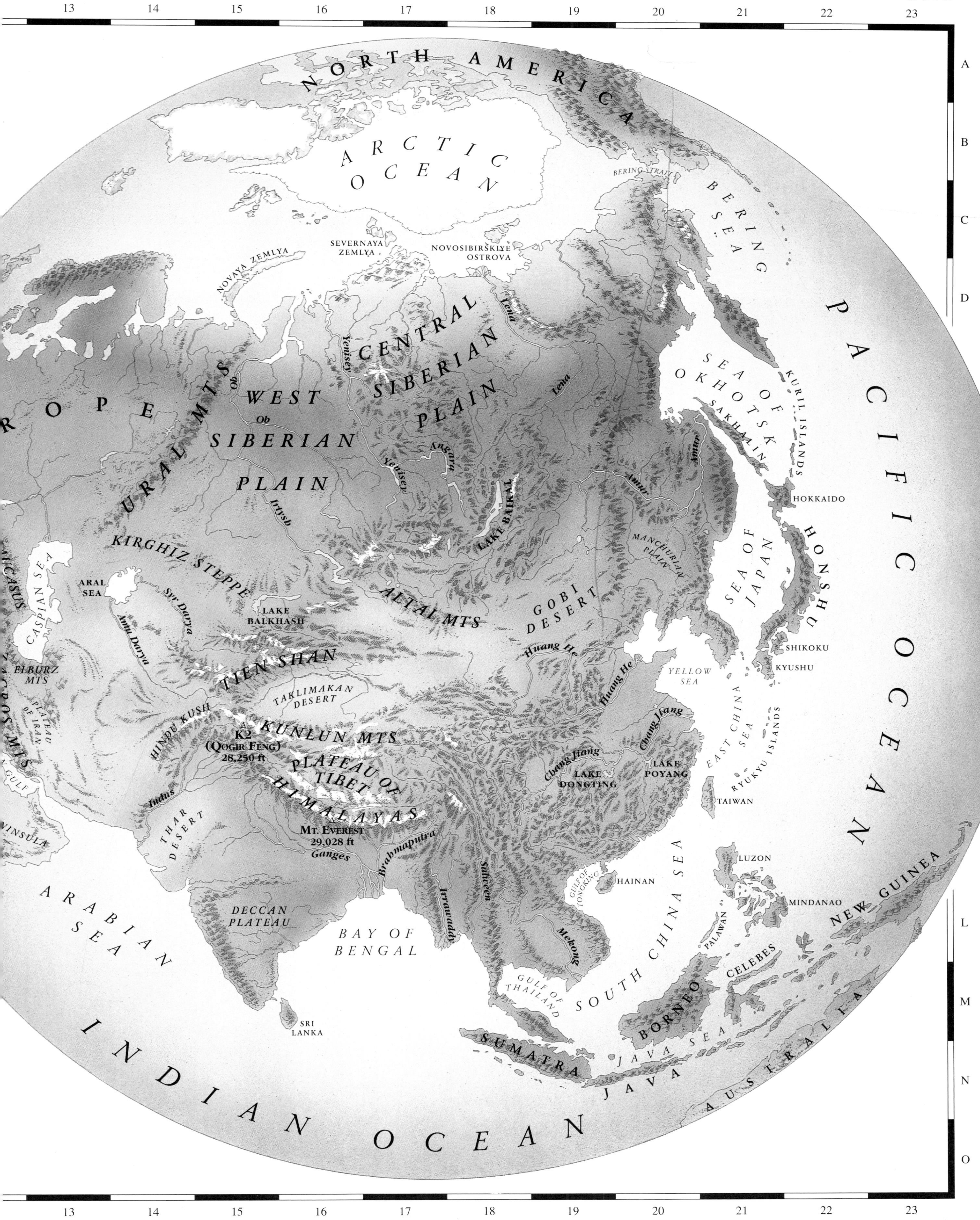

13 14 15 16 17 18 19 20 21 22 23

A
B
C
D

NORTH AMERICA

ARCTIC OCEAN

BERING STRAIT

BERING SEA

NOVAYA ZEMLYA

SEVERNAYA ZEMLYA

NOVOSIBIRSKIYE OSTROVA

Lena

CENTRAL SIBERIAN PLAIN

Yenisey

URAL MTS

WEST SIBERIAN PLAIN

Ob

Ob

Yenisey

Irtysh

Angara

Lena

KURIL ISLANDS

SEA OF OKHOTSK

SAKHALIN

Amur

HOKKAIDO

SEA OF JAPAN

HONSHU

KIRGHIZ STEPPE

ARAL SEA

CAUCASUS

CASPIAN SEA

Syr-Darya

Amu Darya

LAKE BALKHASH

ALTAI MTS

LAKE BAIKAL

MANCHURIAN PLAIN

Amur

GOBI DESERT

Huang He

Huang He

YELLOW SEA

SHIKOKU

KYUSHU

ELBURZ MTS

ZAGROS MTS

PLATEAU OF IRAN

TIEN SHAN

TAKLIMAKAN DESERT

HINDU KUSH

K2 (QOGIR FENG) 28,250 ft

KUNLUN MTS

PLATEAU OF TIBET

HIMALAYAS

MT. EVEREST 29,028 ft

Ganges

Brahmaputra

Indus

THAR DESERT

GULF

PENINSULA

ARABIAN SEA

DECCAN PLATEAU

BAY OF BENGAL

Irrawaddy

Salween

Mekong

Chang Jiang

Chang Jiang

LAKE DONGTING

LAKE POYANG

Chang Jiang

EAST CHINA SEA

RYUKYU ISLANDS

TAIWAN

PACIFIC OCEAN

GULF OF TONGKING

HAINAN

LUZON

PALAWAN

MINDANAO

NEW GUINEA

SOUTH CHINA SEA

GULF OF THAILAND

SRI LANKA

BORNEO

CELEBES

SUMATRA

JAVA SEA

JAVA

AUSTRALIA

INDIAN OCEAN

EUROPE

L
M
N
O

13 14 15 16 17 18 19 20 21 22 23

USSR

THE UNION OF SOVIET SOCIALIST REPUBLICS, or USSR, is the largest country in the world. It is more than twice the size of Canada, the second largest. It stretches about 6,000 miles (9,700 km) from east to west and includes more than one-seventh of the world's total land area.

The USSR spreads across two continents – Europe and Asia. The Ural Mountains divide them, with Europe to the west and Asia to the east. The European part of the USSR occupies only 25 percent of the land area, but about 70 percent of the people live there. To the east lies

Siberia. Much of this region is a huge, uninhabited wilderness with vast pine forests, but it is rich in precious stones and oil. In winter, the temperature in northern Siberia regularly falls below -49°F (-45°C).

The USSR is made up of 15 republics and many more smaller regions. Many different peoples – such as the Georgians, the Uzbeks, and the Russians – live in the USSR. Sometimes the country is called Russia, but this is incorrect: Russia is just one of the republics which make up the USSR.

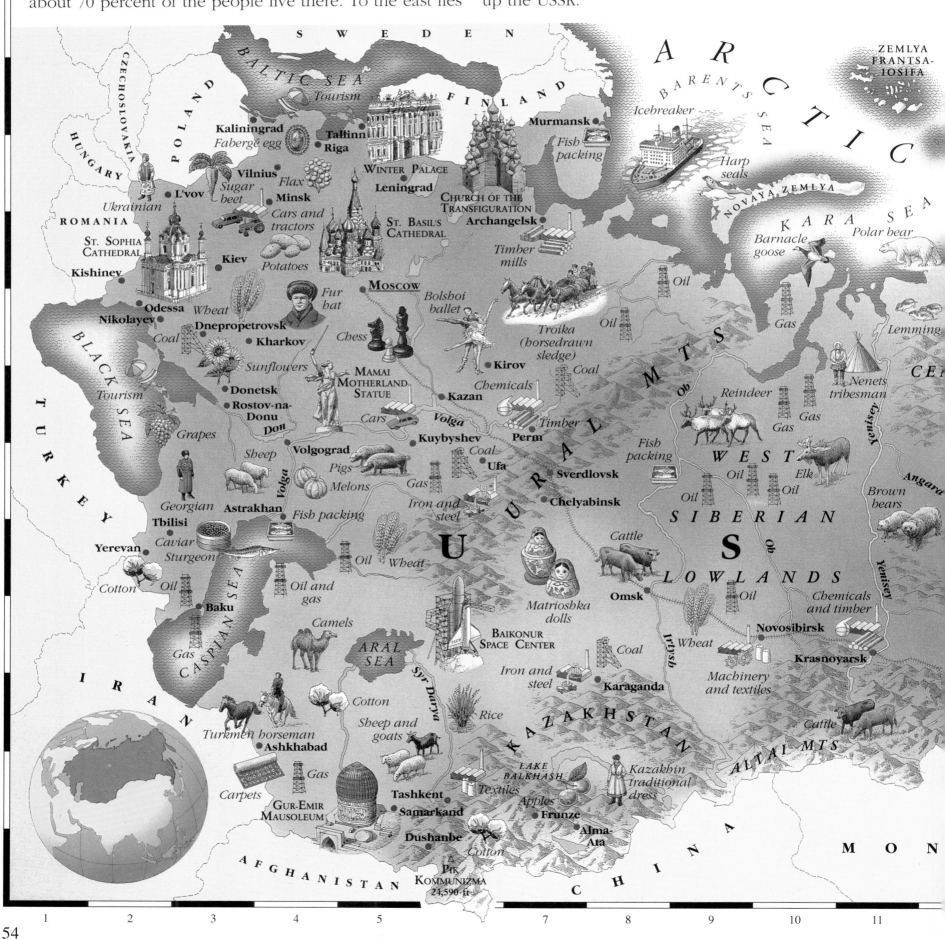

THE KREMLIN

The Kremlin fortress is the oldest part of Moscow. The present walls date from the late 1400s, and inside are cathedrals and palaces. The Great Kremlin Palace was once the home of the Czars (emperors), but now the Supreme Soviet, the government of the USSR, meets there. Outside the Kremlin is Red Square, where a May Day parade is held each year to celebrate the Russian Revolution of 1917. On Red Square is the Lenin Mausoleum, containing the preserved body of Lenin, the "Father of the Revolution."

The Great Kremlin Palace

Lenin Mausoleum

The Cathedral of the Annunciation

FACTS AND FIGURES

The Cathedral of the Annunciation, the Kremlin, Moscow.

Highest mountain: Pik Kommunizma (Communism Peak), 24,590 ft (7,495 m).
Largest lake: Caspian Sea (the largest lake in the world) covers an area of 143,205 sq miles (371,000 sq km).
World's longest canal system: V I Lenin Volga-Baltic Waterway, 1,510 miles (2,430 km) long.
World's longest railway: Trans-Siberian, Moscow to Nakhoda near Vladivostok, 5,864 miles (9,438 km).

Leningrad, which was once called St. Petersburg, was the country's capital city from 1712 until 1918.

USSR
Capital: Moscow
Population: 285,659,000
Area: 8,649,498 sq miles (22,402,200 sq km)
Languages: Russian, many regional languages
Religions: Christian, Moslem, Jewish

UNION REPUBLICS:

ARMENIA
Capital: Yerevan

AZERBAIJAN
Capital: Baku

BYELORUSSIA
Capital: Minsk

ESTONIA
Capital: Tallinn

GEORGIA
Capital: Tbilisi

KAZAKHSTAN
Capital: Alma-Ata

KIRGHIZIA
Capital: Frunze

LATVIA
Capital: Riga

LITHUANIA
Capital: Vilnius

MOLDAVIA
Capital: Kishinev

RUSSIAN SOVIET FEDERATIVE SOCIALIST REPUBLIC (RSFSR)
Capital: Moscow

TAJIKISTAN
Capital: Dushanbe

TURKMENISTAN
Capital: Ashkhabad

UKRAINE
Capital: Kiev

UZBEKISTAN
Capital: Tashkent

Map labels:

0 250 500 750 1000 Kilometers
0 150 300 450 600 Miles

OCEAN

BERING STRAIT

OSTROVA VRANGELYA

SEVERNAYA ZEMLYA

Submarine

Brent goose

LAPTEV SEA

NOVOSIBIRSKIYE OSTROVA

Whales

Gold

Chukchi Eskimo

BERING SEA

Walruses

Yakut tribesman

Evenk reindeer herdsman

EAST SIBERIAN UPLANDS

Furs

Reindeer

RAL SIBERIAN UPLANDS

Wolves

Furs

Diamonds

Diamonds

Coal

Yakutsk

Lena

Yana

Indigirka

Kolyma

Coal

Gold

Gold

KAMCHATKA PENINSULA

Salmon

Fish packing

SEA OF OKHOTSK

Battleship

Fish packing

S R

Furs

Lena

Timber

TRANS SIBERIAN RAILWAY

Manchurian tiger

Salmon

KURIL ISLANDS

Coal

Paper mills

Fish packing

LAKE BAIKAL

Timber mills

Irkutsk

Gold

Iron and steel

Khabarovsk

Chemicals

Buses

CHINA

USSR

Coal

Vladivostok

Fish packing

SEA OF JAPAN

JAPAN

GOLIA

Fishing boat

SOUTHWESTERN ASIA

SOUTHWEST ASIA, also known as the Middle East, lies between three continents – Asia, Africa, and Europe. It contains many varied landscapes and cultures. The countries surrounding the Mediterranean are wetter than the others, and crops such as citrus fruits, olives, and wheat are grown here. To the south stretch the huge deserts of Saudi Arabia. Earlier this century, the world's largest deposits of oil were discovered in the countries around the Persian Gulf. The oilfields in the region now supply the world.

Some of the world's first settled farming communities and towns, such as Jericho in Jordan, grew up in the rich farmlands of the Fertile Crescent, which stretches from the Mediterranean to the area between the Tigris and Euphrates rivers. In recent years, Southwest Asia has been an unsettled region, troubled by a revolution in Iran and a long and bitter war between Iran and Iraq. Civil war in Lebanon has claimed many lives, and there have also been wars between Israel and its Arab neighbors.

CYPRUS

SYRIA

LEBANON

ISRAEL

JORDAN

SAUDI ARABIA

Map labels

ASIA
BLACK SEA
Cherries
Nargle pipe
Tobacco
Tourism
Mosque of Suleiman I
Istanbul
Bursa
Cotton
Shish kebab
PONTINE MTS.
Ankara
Sheep
Goats
AEGEAN SEA
Tourism
Ruins of Ephesus
Carpets
TURKEY
Head of Hercules
Izmir
Konya
Tourism
Whirling dervish
Selemiye Mosque
Adana
Harran domed dwellings
Oi
Bodrum Castle
Grapes
NORTH CYPRUS
Aleppo
Euphrates
Cotton
Sailing
MEDITERRANEAN SEA
NICOSIA
Cedar
SYRIA
Goats
CYPRUS
Beirut
Damascus
Goats
I
Haifa
Silk
Sheep
Tel Aviv-Yafo
Amman
Jerusalem
Oranges
JORDAN
Bedouin tent
SINAI
GULF OF SUEZ
Aqaba
AL HIJAZ
Petra (The Khazneh)
Camels
A N
NAFUD
SAUDI
Coral
Traditional dress
Dates
N E J D
Pearls
Medina
Yanbu
Petrochemicals
RED SEA
The Great Mosque
Mecca
Jiddah
Roses
Sharks
Baboons
Wheat
Barracuda
Coffee

JERUSALEM

Dome of the Rock

Wailing Wall

Jerusalem is a holy place for Christians, Moslems, and Jews, and it is visited by millions of people each year. The Church of the Holy Sepulcher is built where Christians believe Christ was buried. The gold-topped Dome of the Rock is a mosque built where Moslems believe Mohammed ascended into heaven. The Wailing Wall, where Jews go to pray, is all that remains of the Jewish Temple built by King Herod in the 1st century BC.

13 14 15 16 17 18 19 20 21 22 23

Map labels

TURKEY

IRAQ

IRAN

Tea

Bears

Tobacco

MT. ARARAT 16,804 ft

LAKE VAN

Oil

Apples

Melons

Tabriz

Kurdish dress

Rice

Mosul

Oil

HAYDAR KHANAH MOSQUE

BAKHTARAN

BAGHDAD

Tigris

Dates

ZIGGURAT AT UR

Oil

Arab marsh reed house

Basra

Abadan

Ahvaz

Chemicals

Textiles

Oil

KUWAIT

Oil

Oil

Silk

Carpets

Qom

LAKE NAMAK

TEHRAN

THE ROYAL MOSQUE

Isfahan

Caviar

Tea

Sturgeon

ELBURZ MTS

Traditional dress

Pigeon towers

Cotton

PERSEPOLIS (PALACE STAIRCASE)

Shiraz

Mashhad

Turquoise

Goats

Sheep

BAM

Gas

Gas

AFGHANISTAN

PAKISTAN

U S S R

CASPIAN SEA

Oil

Cattle

Petrochemicals

Oil

Oil

PERSIAN GULF

Al Jubayl

Oil

Oil

Oil

QATAR

DOHA

Oil tanker

Oil

Dubai

ABU DHABI

Oil

UNITED ARAB EMIRATES

Dates

Khanjar (Arab dagger)

Oil

Oil

Incense burner

Kummas Omani (embroidered cap)

Oil

Oil

MUSCAT

Sardines

GULF OF OMAN

Dhow (Arab boat)

STRAIT OF HORMUZ

ARABIA

Yashmak (face veil)

AD DAHNA

RIYADH

Arab horses

Falconry

ARABIAN DESERT

Sand dunes 700 ft

JIZAN DAM

RUB AL KHALI

Arabian oryx

OMAN

Ancient painted house

Camels

Frankincense (Boswellia tree)

YEMEN

SAN'A'

Dates

Cotton

Aden

Dhow (Arab boat)

Oil tanker

ARABIAN SEA

OMAN

KUWAIT

BAHRAIN

YEMEN

QATAR

UNITED ARAB EMIRATES

Scale

600 Kilometers / 400 Miles

0 150 300 450 600 Kilometers
0 100 200 300 400 Miles

Facts and Figures

FACTS AND FIGURES

Dhow (Arab boat) off the Yemen coast.

Largest city: Tehran (Iran), 6,400,000.

Hottest capital: Riyadh, in Saudi Arabia, is the hottest capital city in the world, with average July temperatures of over 104°F (40°C).

Sand dunes in the Rub al Khali (The Empty Quarter) in Saudi Arabia. Dunes are formed by the wind, which blows the sand into mounds.

BAHRAIN
Capital: Al Manamah
Area: 262 sq miles (678 sq km)

CYPRUS
Capital: Nicosia
Area: 3,571 sq miles (9,251 sq km)

IRAN
Capital: Tehran
Area: 636,297 sq miles (1,648,000 sq km)

IRAQ
Capital: Baghdad
Area: 169,235 sq miles (438,317 sq km)

ISRAEL
Capital: Jerusalem
Area: 8,017 sq miles (20,770 sq km)

JORDAN
Capital: Amman
Area: 37,737 sq miles (97,740 sq km)

KUWAIT
Capital: Kuwait
Area: 6,879 sq miles (17,818 sq km)

LEBANON
Capital: Beirut
Area: 4,015 sq miles (10,400 sq km)

OMAN
Capital: Muscat
Area: 82,030 sq miles (212,457 sq km)

QATAR
Capital: Doha
Area: 4,247 sq miles (11,000 sq km)

SAUDI ARABIA
Capital: Riyadh
Area: 830,001 sq miles (2,149,690 sq km)

SYRIA
Capital: Damascus
Area: 71,500 sq miles (185,180 sq km)

TURKEY
Capital: Ankara
Area: 300,948 sq miles (779,452 sq km)

UNITED ARAB EMIRATES
Capital: Abu Dhabi
Area: 32,278 sq miles (83,600 sq km)

YEMEN
Capital: San'a'
Area: 203,850 sq miles (527,968 sq km)

A B C D E F G H I J K L M N O

SOUTHERN ASIA

THE LARGEST COUNTRY in Southern Asia is India, and the region is often called the "Indian subcontinent". Over one billion people live in Southern Asia – around 22 percent of the world's total population.

Most people in Southern Asia live in the wetter areas on the coasts and on the fertile plains of the Indus and Ganges rivers. Nearly three-quarters of the people earn their living from farming. Water is vital, and farmers depend on the monsoon rains, which fall between May and November. The most important crop is rice.

India was united in the 16th and 17th centuries under the Mogul emperors. Then, in the 18th century, the country became part of the British Empire. India gained independence from Britain in 1947, when it was divided into two countries with different religions: Moslem Pakistan and Hindu India. In 1971 the eastern part of Pakistan became a separate country, called Bangladesh.

Today Pakistan and India are the most industrial countries in Southern Asia. Pakistan has textile, food processing, and chemical industries. India produces oil, coal, iron ore, manganese, and copper, and has a variety of industries, including iron and steel, car manufacturing, and computers.

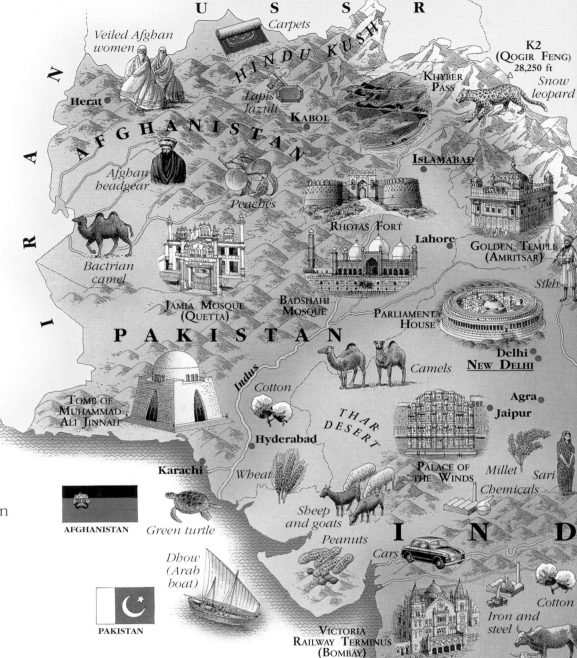

THE TAJ MAHAL

The Taj Mahal was built near Agra in northern India by the Mogul Emperor Shah Jehan as a burial place for his wife, the Empress Mumtaz Mahal. It was built between 1630 and 1650 and about 20,000 laborers worked on the building. The Taj Mahal is made of white marble, which was brought 310 miles (500 km) from Rajasthan. The interior is decorated with precious and semiprecious stones.

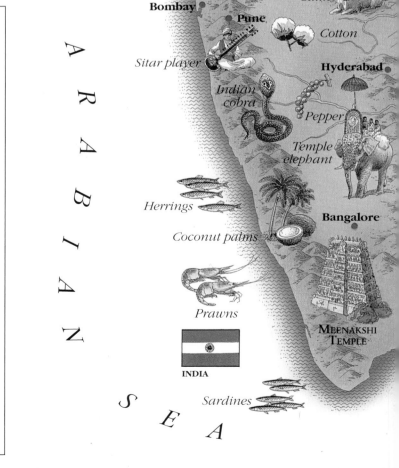

MOUNTAIN PEAKS IN THE HIMALAYAS

MT. EVEREST
29,028 ft

KANCHENJUNGA
28,170 ft

MAKALU I
27,824 ft

DHAULAGIRI
26,810 ft

NANGA PARBAT
26,660 ft

FACTS AND FIGURES

Fishermen at Negombo, Sri Lanka.

Largest cities:
Calcutta (India), 11,100,000;
Bombay (India), 9,950,000;
Delhi (India), 7,200,000;
Karachi (Pakistan), 5,300,000;
Madras (India), 4,475,000;
Dhaka (Bangladesh), 3,430,312.

Longest river:
Indus, 1,800 miles (2,896 km).

Largest island: Sri Lanka,
25,325 sq miles (65,610 sq km).

Highest mountains:
Everest (Nepal-China), 29,028 ft
(8,848 m); K2 (Qogir Feng)
(Pakistan-China), 28,250 ft
(8,611 m); Kanchenjunga (India-
Nepal), 28,170 ft (8,586 m).

**World's heaviest recorded
annual rainfall:** Cherrapunji, in
northeast India, received 1,042 in
(26.4 m) of rain between August
1860 and July 1861.

*Many Nepalese farmers keep yaks,
which are used as pack animals. They
also provide milk, meat, and wool.*

AFGHANISTAN
Capital: Kabol
Area: 251,792 sq miles (652,090 sq km)
Population: 17,375,000

BANGLADESH
Capital: Dhaka
Area: 55,602 sq miles (143,998 sq km)
Population: 108,851,000

BHUTAN
Capital: Thimphu
Area: 18,148 sq miles (47,000 sq km)
Population: 1,373,000

BURMA (MYANMAR)
Capital: Rangoon (Yangon)
Area: 261,237 sq miles (676,552 sq km)
Population: 40,162,000

INDIA
Capital: New Delhi
Area: 1,269,437 sq miles (3,287,590 sq km)
Population: 813,990,000

NEPAL
Capital: Kathmandu
Area: 54,365 sq miles (140,797 sq km)
Population: 18,053,000

PAKISTAN
Capital: Islamabad
Area: 307,396 sq miles (796,095 sq km)
Population: 105,677,000

SRI LANKA
Capital: Colombo
Area: 25,334 sq miles (65,610 sq km)
Population: 16,565,000

CHINA

Yaks

MT. EVEREST
29,028 ft

Red panda

NEPAL

KATHMANDU

HIMALAYAS

THIMPHU

Picking tea

BHUTAN

Sugarcane

Rice

Indian rhinoceros

Rubies

Jade

Hauling teak logs

Dhoti (loincloth)

Ox cart

Ganges

Pedal rickshaw

VICTORIA MEMORIAL

DHAKA

BANGLADESH

BURMA (MYANMAR)

Opium poppy

INDIA

Tiger

Coal

Rice

Calcutta

Mandalay

LINGARAJA TEMPLE

Tobacco

Fishing

PAGAN TEMPLE (ANANDA)

Leg rower

"Giraffe" necked woman of Padaung

Hindu dancer

BANGLADESH

NEPAL

SHWE DAGON PADOGA

RANGOON (YANGON)

Buddhist monks

Krishna

BHUTAN

Rubber trees

Mackerel

BAY OF BENGAL

BURMA (MYANMAR)

THAILAND

Madras

ANDAMAN ISLANDS (INDIA)

Lobster

Outrigger fishing boat

SRI LANKA

Picking tea

SRI LANKA

Coconut palms

COLOMBO

NICOBAR ISLANDS (INDIA)

SOUTHEASTERN ASIA

SOUTHEASTERN ASIA is made up of a narrow strip of mainland and thousands of islands. The country of Indonesia consists of over 13,000 islands and has the fifth largest population in the world. Most Indonesians live on the island of Java. The Philippines is a collection of more than 7,000 islands. In contrast to these scatterings of islands is the tiny oil-rich country of Brunei. The sultan (ruler) of Brunei is said to be the richest person in the world..

The climate in this region is hot and wet throughout the year, with very heavy rains during the monsoon season. Thick forests cover much of the area, though many trees have been cleared for timber and for growing crops such as rice, tobacco, pineapples, and rubber.

From the 16th to 19th centuries most of the region was colonized by Europeans. This century many wars were fought between the local people and the colonizing countries, and today all the countries are independent again.

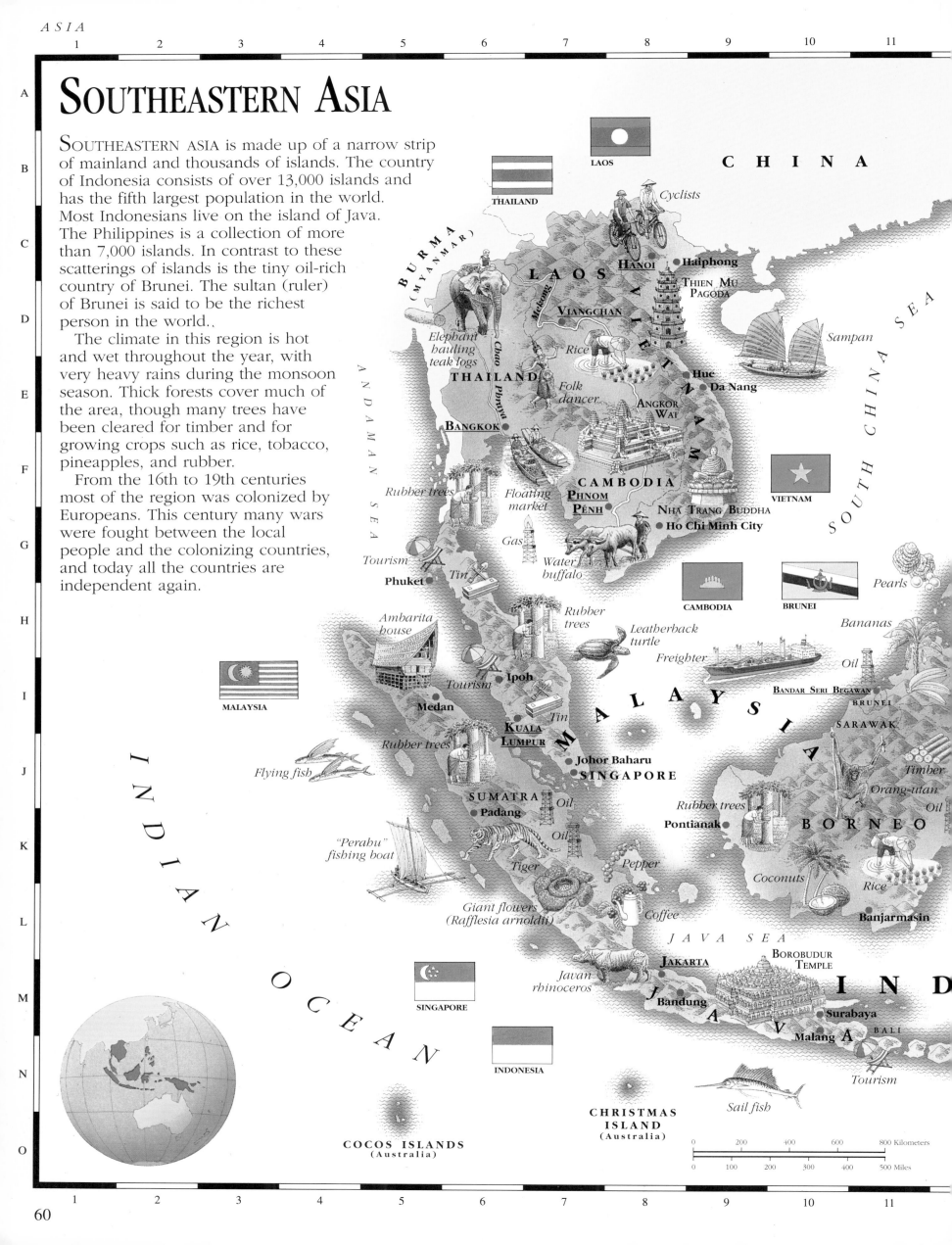

LAOS

THAILAND

CHINA

BURMA (MYANMAR)

Cyclists

LAOS

HANOI •Haiphong

THIEN MU PAGODA

Elephant hauling teak logs

VIANGCHAN

Rice

Mekong

THAILAND

Chao Phraya

Folk dancer

Hue Da Nang

ANGKOR WAT

Sampan

SOUTH CHINA SEA

BANGKOK

CAMBODIA

PHNOM PENH

NHA TRANG BUDDHA

Ho Chi Minh City

VIETNAM

ANDAMAN SEA

Rubber trees

Floating market

Gas

Tourism

Phuket Tin

Water buffalo

CAMBODIA BRUNEI

Pearls

Bananas

Ambarita house

Rubber trees

Leatherback turtle

Freighter

Oil

MALAYSIA

Tourism Ipoh

MALAYSIA

Medan

SARAWAK

Rubber trees

Bandar Seri Begawan

BRUNEI

Timber

INDIAN OCEAN

KUALA LUMPUR

Tin

Orang-utan

Oil

Flying fish

Johor Baharu

SINGAPORE

BORNEO

SUMATRA

Padang Oil

Rubber trees

Pontianak

"Perahu" fishing boat

Oil

Coconuts

Rice

Tiger

Pepper

Banjarmasin

Giant flowers (Rafflesia arnoldii)

Coffee

JAVA SEA

BOROBUDUR TEMPLE

SINGAPORE

Javan rhinoceros

JAKARTA

IND

Bandung

JAVA

SINGAPORE

Surabaya

BALI

Malang

INDONESIA

CHRISTMAS ISLAND (Australia)

Sail fish

Tourism

COCOS ISLANDS (Australia)

Scale:
0 200 400 600 800 Kilometers
0 100 200 300 400 500 Miles

FACTS AND FIGURES

Planting rice in Malaysia. Seedlings are transplanted to a flooded field after they have grown in a nursery.

Longest river:
Mekong, 2,600 miles (4,184 km).

Longest name in the world:
The Thai name for Bangkok is Krungthep maha nakorn, amarn rattanakosindra, mahindrayudhya, mahadilok pop noparatana rajdhani mahasathan, amorn piman avatarn satit, sakkatultiya visanukarn prasit.

Largest cities:
Jakarta (Indonesia), 8,600,000; Manila (Philippines), 6,800,000; Bangkok (Thailand), 6,450,000; Ho Chi Minh City (Vietnam, previously called Saigon), 3,100,000.

Highest mountain: Puncak Jaya (Indonesia), 16,503 ft (5,030 m).

Largest island: New Guinea, 312,085 sq miles (808,510 sq km).

BRUNEI
Capital: Bandar Seri Begawan
Area: 2,225 sq miles (5,765 sq km)
Population: 243,000
Languages: Malay, English
Religion: Moslem

CAMBODIA
Capital: Phnom Pénh
Area: 69,881 sq miles (181,035 sq km)
Population: 5,728,771
Language: Khmer
Religion: Buddhist

INDONESIA
Capital: Jakarta
Area: 735,412 sq miles (1,904,569 sq km)
Population: 174,832,000
Language: Indonesian
Religion: Moslem

LAOS
Capital: Viangchan
Area: 91,435 sq miles (236,800 sq km)
Population: 3,879,000
Languages: Lao, French
Religion: Buddhist

MALAYSIA
Capital: Kuala Lumpur
Area: 127,326 sq miles (329,749 sq km)
Population: 16,921,000
Languages: Malay, English, Chinese
Religions: Moslem, Buddhist

PAPUA NEW GUINEA
Capital: Port Moresby
Area: 178,716 sq miles (462,840 sq km)
Population: 3,804,000
Languages: English, numerous others
Religion: Christian

PHILIPPINES
Capital: Manila
Area: 115,839 sq miles (300,000 sq km)
Population: 59,686,000
Languages: Pilipino, English, Spanish
Religions: Christian, Moslem

SINGAPORE
Capital: Singapore City
Area: 239 sq miles (618 sq km)
Population: 2,639,000
Languages: Malay, Chinese, English
Religions: Taoist, Buddhist

THAILAND
Capital: Bangkok
Area: 198,129 sq miles (513,115 sq km)
Population: 54,469,000
Language: Thai
Religion: Buddhist

VIETNAM
Capital: Hanoi
Area: 127,252 sq miles (329,558 sq km)
Population: 66,682,000
Languages: Vietnamese, French, Chinese
Religion: Buddhist

SINGAPORE

Singapore is a small island, just 25 miles (40 km) long by 15.5 miles (25 km) wide. It is an independent nation and one of the world's most important ports and trading centers. Many different races live in Singapore. Three-quarters of the population are Chinese, with smaller numbers of Malays and Indians. The remainder are Europeans, Arabs, or Japanese. These people all celebrate different festivals, making Singapore a lively and colorful place throughout the year.

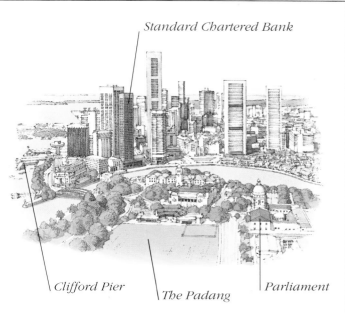

Standard Chartered Bank
Clifford Pier
The Padang
Parliament

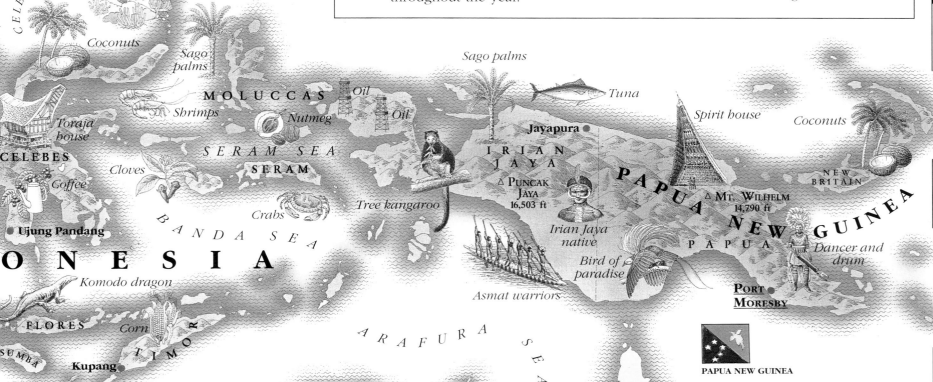

TAIWAN

MANILA

LUZON

Rice terraces

PACIFIC OCEAN

PHILIPPINES

Sugarcane

Cebu

PHILIPPINES

Coral reefs

Zamboanga

MINDANAO

Davao

Monkey-eating eagle

Vinta boat

Coral reefs

CELEBES SEA

Coconuts

Sago palms

Sago palms

MOLUCCAS

Oil

Shrimps

Nutmeg

Oil

Tuna

Spirit house

Coconuts

Toraja house

SERAM SEA

SERAM

Jayapura

IRIAN JAYA

PAPUA NEW GUINEA

NEW BRITAIN

CELEBES

Cloves

△ PUNCAK JAYA 16,503 ft

△ MT. WILHELM 14,790 ft

Coffee

Tree kangaroo

Irian Jaya native

PAPUA

Dancer and drum

Ujung Pandang

Crabs

BANDA SEA

Bird of paradise

ONESIA

Komodo dragon

Asmat warriors

PORT MORESBY

FLORES

Corn

TIMOR

Kupang

ARAFURA SEA

PAPUA NEW GUINEA

SUMBA

TIMOR SEA

AUSTRALIA

CHINA AND NORTHEASTERN ASIA

MORE PEOPLE live in China than in any other country. China has over one billion inhabitants, and one person in every five in the world is Chinese. China is also the world's third largest country, after the USSR and Canada. Most people live in the east of China, where the climate is wet and the land is good for farming. In most places the land is owned by each village, and everyone works on it together, sharing the harvest.

Tibet lies in the highlands of southwest China at an average height of 14,800 ft (4,500 m) above sea level. This is higher than most mountains in Europe and the United States. The Himalayas, the world's highest mountains, stretch along the border with India.

After a long civil war in China, a communist government was formed in 1949, led by Mao Zedong. The defeated nationalists set up a rival Republic of China on the small island of Taiwan, which is still independent. The small province of Hong Kong is at present a British colony, but it will become part of China in 1997. In Korea, a war was fought between communist and non-communist forces. Korea is now divided into two countries, North and South Korea.

THE FORBIDDEN CITY

On one side of the central square in China's capital city, Beijing (Peking), is Tiananmen Gate, the Gate of Heavenly Peace. Through it lies the old city where the Chinese emperors had their court from 1421 to 1911. It was known as the Forbidden City because ordinary people were not allowed to enter, but today it is open to the public. At its heart the Imperial Palace is surrounded by a high wall and a water-filled moat.

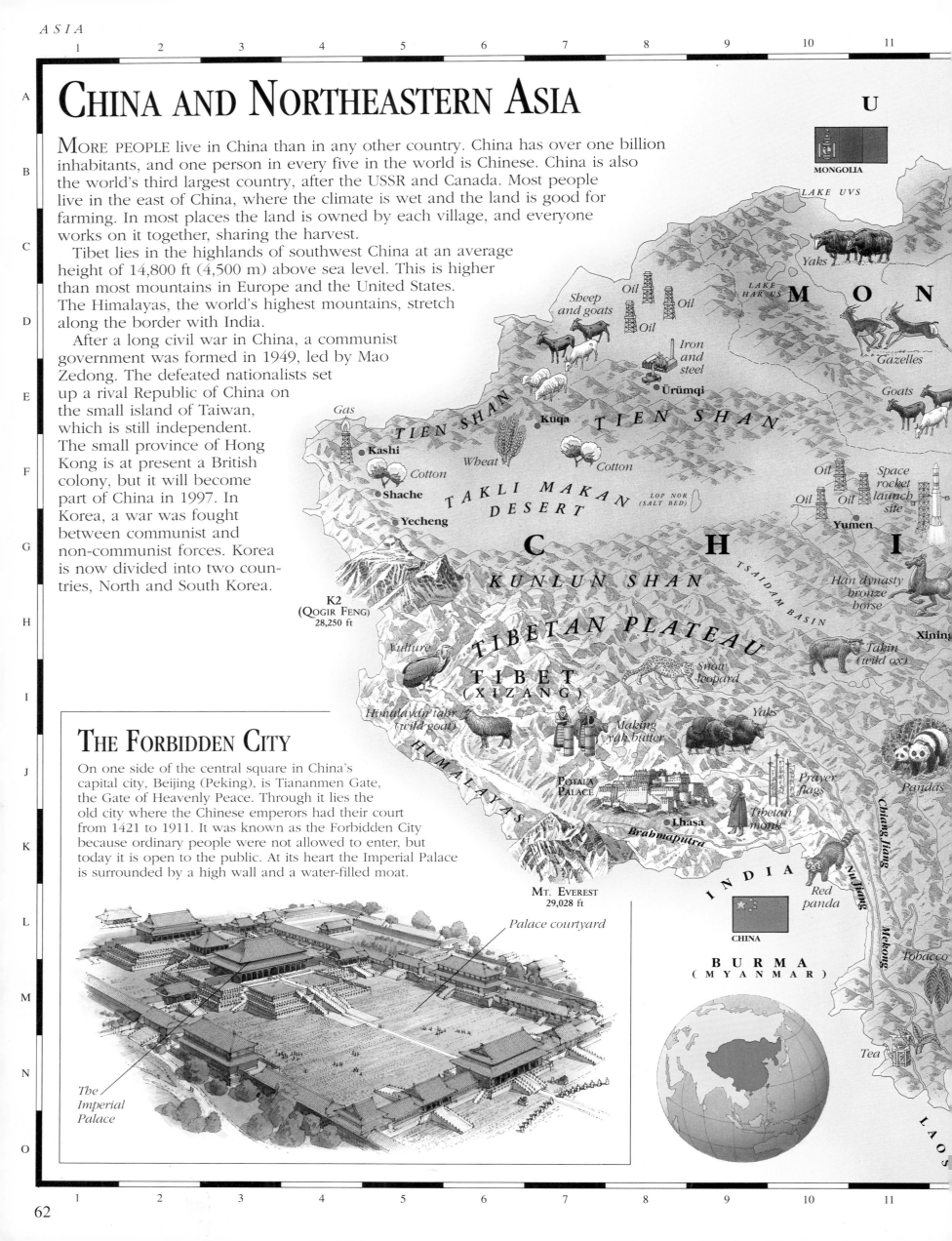

U

MONGOLIA

LAKE UVS

LAKE HAR US

M O N

Yaks

Sheep and goats

Oil
Oil
Oil

Gazelles

Iron and steel

Goats

Ürümqi

Gas

TIEN SHAN

Kuqa

TIEN SHAN

Kashi

Wheat

Cotton

Cotton

Oil

Space rocket launch site

Shache

TAKLI MAKAN DESERT

LOP NOR (SALT BED)

Oil

Oil

Yumen

Yecheng

C   H

I

TSAIDAM BASIN

Han dynasty bronze horse

KUNLUN SHAN

K2 (QOGIR FENG) 28,250 ft

Vulture

TIBETAN PLATEAU

Takin (wild ox)

Xining

Snow leopard

TIBET (XIZANG)

Himalayan tahr (wild goat)

Making yak butter

Yaks

HIMALAYAS

POTALA PALACE

Prayer flags

Pandas

Lhasa

Tibetan monk

Brahmaputra

MT. EVEREST 29,028 ft

INDIA

CHINA

Red panda

Chiang Jiang

Nu Jiang

Palace courtyard

The Imperial Palace

BURMA (MYANMAR)

Mekong

Tobacco

Tea

LAOS

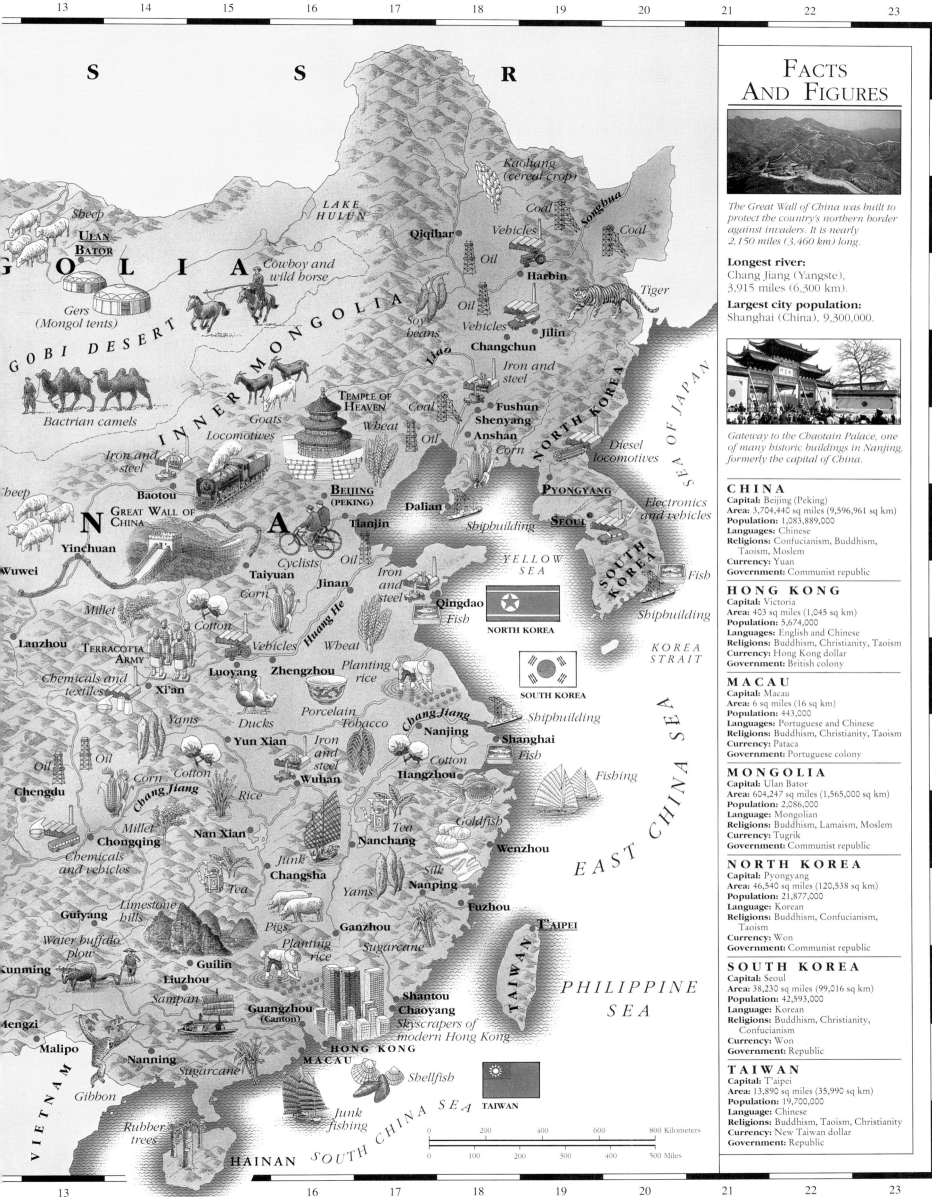

13 **14** **15** **16** **17** **18** **19** **20** **21** **22** **23**

S S S R

A

GOLIA

LAKE HULUN

Kaoliang (cereal crop)

B

Sheep

ULAN BATOR

Cowboy and wild horse

Gers (Mongol tents)

Coal

Songhua

Coal

C

Qiqihar

Vehicles

Oil

Harbin

GOBI DESERT

Oil

Tiger

D

Bactrian camels

INNER MONGOLIA

Soy beans

Vehicles

Jilin

Changchun

Iron and steel

E

Goats

Locomotives

TEMPLE OF HEAVEN

Wheat

Coal

Oil

Fushun

Shenyang

Anshan

NORTH KOREA

SEA OF JAPAN

Diesel locomotives

F

Iron and steel

Baotou

N

GREAT WALL OF CHINA

Yinchuan

Corn

PYONGYANG

SEOUL

Electronics and vehicles

G

Sheep

Wuwei

A

BEIJING (PEKING)

Dalian

Tianjin

Shipbuilding

SOUTH KOREA

Cyclists

Oil

Taiyuan

Millet

Corn

Jinan

Iron and steel

YELLOW SEA

Fish

H

Lanzhou

TERRACOTTA ARMY

Cotton

Huang He

Qingdao

Fish

NORTH KOREA

Shipbuilding

KOREA STRAIT

Chemicals and textiles

Vehicles

Wheat

I

Xi'an

Luoyang **Zhengzhou**

Planting rice

SOUTH KOREA

Yams

Ducks

Porcelain

Chang Jiang

Shipbuilding

J

Oil

Oil

Corn

Cotton

Tobacco

Nanjing

Shanghai

Fish

Chengdu

Chang Jiang

Rice

Iron and steel

Wuhan

Cotton

Hangzhou

EAST CHINA SEA

Fishing

K

Millet

Chongqing

Nan Xian

Tea

Goldfish

Nanchang

Wenzhou

Chemicals and vehicles

Junk

Changsha

Yams

Silk

Nanping

L

Limestone hills

Guiyang

Pigs

Planting rice

Fuzhou

Water buffalo plow

Guilin

Ganzhou

Sugarcane

T'AIPEI

M

Kunming

Liuzhou

Sampan

TAIWAN

PHILIPPINE SEA

Mengzi

Shantou

Chaoyang

Skyscrapers of modern Hong Kong

N

Malipo

Nanning

Guangzhou (Canton)

HONG KONG

MACAU

VIETNAM

Sugarcane

Shellfish

TAIWAN

Gibbon

Junk fishing

SOUTH CHINA SEA

O

Rubber trees

HAINAN

0 200 400 600 800 Kilometers

0 100 200 300 400 500 Miles

FACTS AND FIGURES

The Great Wall of China was built to protect the country's northern border against invaders. It is nearly 2,150 miles (3,460 km) long.

Longest river: Chang Jiang (Yangste), 3,915 miles (6,300 km).

Largest city population: Shanghai (China), 9,300,000.

Gateway to the Chaotain Palace, one of many historic buildings in Nanjing, formerly the capital of China.

CHINA
Capital: Beijing (Peking)
Area: 3,704,440 sq miles (9,596,961 sq km)
Population: 1,083,889,000
Languages: Chinese
Religions: Confucianism, Buddhism, Taoism, Moslem
Currency: Yuan
Government: Communist republic

HONG KONG
Capital: Victoria
Area: 403 sq miles (1,045 sq km)
Population: 5,674,000
Languages: English and Chinese
Religions: Buddhism, Christianity, Taoism
Currency: Hong Kong dollar
Government: British colony

MACAU
Capital: Macau
Area: 6 sq miles (16 sq km)
Population: 443,000
Languages: Portuguese and Chinese
Religions: Buddhism, Christianity, Taoism
Currency: Pataca
Government: Portuguese colony

MONGOLIA
Capital: Ulan Bator
Area: 604,247 sq miles (1,565,000 sq km)
Population: 2,086,000
Language: Mongolian
Religions: Buddhism, Lamaism, Moslem
Currency: Tugrik
Government: Communist republic

NORTH KOREA
Capital: Pyongyang
Area: 46,540 sq miles (120,538 sq km)
Population: 21,877,000
Language: Korean
Religions: Buddhism, Confucianism, Taoism
Currency: Won
Government: Communist republic

SOUTH KOREA
Capital: Seoul
Area: 38,230 sq miles (99,016 sq km)
Population: 42,593,000
Language: Korean
Religions: Buddhism, Christianity, Confucianism
Currency: Won
Government: Republic

TAIWAN
Capital: T'aipei
Area: 13,890 sq miles (35,990 sq km)
Population: 19,700,000
Language: Chinese
Religions: Buddhism, Taoism, Christianity
Currency: New Taiwan dollar
Government: Republic

JAPAN

JAPAN is made up of four main islands – called Hokkaido, Honshu, Shikoku, and Kyushu – and thousands of smaller ones. The country lies to the east of the main part of Asia. This is an area where two plates of the earth's crust meet, making earthquakes common. Nearly three-quarters of the country is mountainous and wooded. There is little land suitable for agriculture, but what there is is farmed very efficiently. The main crop is rice. Because much of the land cannot be farmed for food, the Japanese eat a lot of fish, and Japan catches more fish than any other nation.

Japan's 122 million people live on the small amount of flat land, mostly on the coasts. In these populated areas there is a very dense concentration of people and activity. Most of the people live in the great cities on the south coast of Honshu island, such as Nagoya, Tokyo, and Osaka.

In the last 40 years Japan has become one of the world's most important industrial nations. This is all the more remarkable because the oil and most of the raw materials that are needed to make the goods have to be imported into the country. Japanese cars, electrical goods, ships, cameras, and many other products are exported all over the world.

KYOTO

Kyoto (or Heian) lies on the island of Honshu. It is one of Japan's largest cities and an important cultural center. For more than 1,000 years it was the capital city of Japan. It has many historic treasures, including shrines, temples, gardens, and ancient buildings. It is Japan's most popular tourist center and about 20 million people visit the city every year.

Mt. Yotei 6,210 ft

JAPAN

Map labels

Skyscrapers of modern Tokyo

Tuna

Electronics

Hitachi

Macaque

TOKYO

Electronics

Kawasaki
Yokohama

BRONZE BUDDHA (KAMAKURA)

IZU-SHOTO ISLANDS

Shizuoka

Skiing

Nagano

Cherry blossom

Mt. Fuji 12,388 ft

Serow

Tea terraces

Toyama

Cars

Nagoya

NAGOYA CASTLE

Bullet train

Pearls

Sumo wrestler

Fukui

Kyoto

GOLD PAVILION

Iron and steel

Kobe

Osaka

Shipbuilding

Citrus fruits

Sardines

Terraced rice fields

Fishing boats

Squid

Tottori

Shinto dignitary

Okayama

SHIKOKU

Kochi

Satsumas

Crab

Squid

Oil tanker

Shrimps

Loggerhead turtle

Tofu (bean curd)

Miyazaki

Rice planting

Sweet potatoes

Kumamoto

KYUSHU

Iron and steel

Chemicals

Kagoshima

OSUMI ISLANDS

Octopus

Shellfish

GOTO ISLANDS

Nagasaki

Fukuoka

Kitakyushu

IKI

Pottery

TSUSHIMA ISLANDS

Anchovies

Mackerel

Kabuki theatre

Shinto shrine

Torii gate

Hiroshima

MATSUYAMA CASTLE

OKI ISLANDS

SEA OF JAPAN

EAST CHINA SEA

PACIFIC OCEAN

NIPPON

200 Kilometers / *125 Miles*
150 — 100
100 — 75
50 — 50
— 25
0 — 0

Facts and Figures box

Tokyo, Japan's capital, and a major industrial port.

Temple statue at Nikko, Honshu.

JAPAN
Capital: Tokyo
Area: 145,835 sq miles (377,801 sq km)
Population: 122,433,000
Language: Japanese
Religions: Shintoism, Buddhism
Currency: Yen

FACTS AND FIGURES

World's largest fishing fleet: Japan catches around 14 percent of the total world catch – more than any other country. Each Japanese person eats an average of 65 lbs (30 kg) of fish a year.

World's tallest lighthouse: The steel lighthouse in Yokohama, Japan is 348 ft (106 m) high. It can be seen from 20 miles (32 km) away.

Food: Only 15 percent of the land, mostly on the coastal plains, can be farmed. But despite this, Japan is 70 percent self-sufficient in food.

World's top oil importer: Japan. The *Seawise Giant*, a Japanese tanker built in 1981, is the largest tanker in the world. It is almost 547 yards (500 m) long and can carry 622,630 U.S. tons of crude oil.

Four largest islands: Honshu, Hokkaido, Kyushu, Shikoku. There are also about 4,000 small islands.

Highest mountain: Mt Fuji, 12,388 ft (3,776 m).

Main ports: Tokyo, Yokohama, Osaka, and Kobe.

Wettest area: All of Japan has high rainfall, but the wettest place is the southernmost island of Kyushu, where average rainfall reaches over 86.6 in (2,200 mm) per year.

Coldest area: Hokkaido has average winter temperatures of 14°F (-10°C).

Longest railway tunnel in the world: The Seikan Rail Tunnel in Japan runs for 33.46 miles (53.85 km) between Tappi Saki on Honshu island and Fukushima on Hokkaido.

A typical Japanese garden in Hiroshima.

Oil tanker

Largest cities: Tokyo, 27,700,000; Osaka, 16,450,000; Nagoya, 4,800,000; Yokohama, 2,992,926; Sapporo, 1,900,000; Fukuoka, 1,750,000; Kyoto, 1,479,218; Kobe, 1,410,834.

AFRICA

The Muhammad Ali mosque in Cairo, Egypt.

AFRICA, the world's second largest continent, stretches about 2,500 miles (4,000 km) north and south of the equator. It is the warmest of all the continents. The only permanent snow and ice are found on the peaks of the highest mountains, such as Mount Kenya and Mount Kilimanjaro. In the regions near the equator, the hot and wet climate supports the dense jungle vegetation of the tropical rain forest. Today much of the forest has been cleared for farming and timber.

Moving away from the equator, the climate becomes increasingly dry, and the forest gives way to tropical grassland, called savannah. For thousands of years the savannah has supported huge herds of plant-eating animals – gazelles, wildebeest, zebras, elephants, and giraffes – along with the predators who hunt and feed on them – lions, leopards, and hyenas. Today farming has greatly reduced the size of the herds, and some animals, such as the African elephant, are in danger of being wiped out forever.

Still farther to the north and south lie the great deserts, where the climate is so dry that few plants

Open cast mining in South Africa.

and animals can survive. Northern Africa is dominated by the Sahara, the world's largest desert. In the south lie the Kalahari and Namib deserts.

Africa is an immense plateau, broken by a few mountain ranges. In some areas a narrow coastal plain stretches along the edge of the plateau. Cutting across East Africa is the Great Rift Valley, with its many lakes and volcanoes. This long valley was formed centuries ago when land slipped down between huge cracks in the earth's crust. Some scientists believe that the land east of the Rift Valley will eventually break away from Africa and become a new continent, just as the Red Sea marks the place where Arabia once split away from the rest of Africa.

Off the east coast of Africa lies the island of Madagascar, which broke away from Africa over 50 million years ago. Because of the island's isolation, unique plants and animals have evolved there. Twenty species of lemur, an animal distantly related to the monkey, are only found there.

Equatorial vegetation in Cameroon.

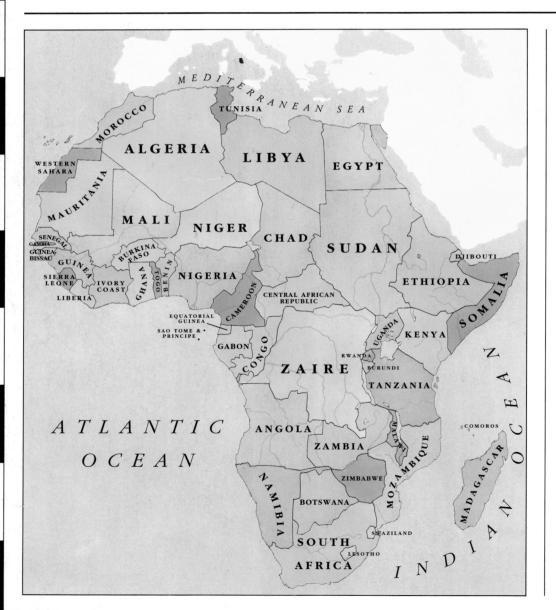

FACTS ABOUT AFRICA

Area: 11,712,434 sq miles (30,335,000 sq km).

Population: 613,566,000.

Number of independent countries: 52 (the most on any continent).

Largest countries: Sudan, 967,500 sq miles (2,500,000 sq km); Algeria, 919,597 sq miles (2,381,741 sq km).

Most populated countries: Nigeria, 110,131,000; Egypt, 51,447,000; Ethiopia, 46,144,000.

Largest cities: Cairo (Egypt), 9,300,000; Alexandria (Egypt), 3,350,000; Kinshasa (Zaire), 3,000,000.

Highest mountains: Kilimanjaro (Tanzania), 19,344 ft (5,896 m); Mt. Kenya (Kenya), 17,057 ft (5,199 m); Mt. Margherita (Uganda-Zaire), 16,763 ft (5,110 m); Ras Dashen (Ethiopia), 15,158 ft (4,620 m).

Longest rivers: Nile, 4,145 miles (6,670 km), the longest in the world; Congo, 2,900 miles (4,667 km); Niger, 2,600 miles (4,184 km); Zambezi, 1,700 miles (2,735 km).

Largest lakes: Lake Victoria, 26,800 sq miles (69,400 sq km); Lake Tanganyika, 12,102 sq miles (32,900 sq km); Lake Nyasa, 11,100 sq miles (28,750 sq km); Lake Chad, area varies from 4,000-10,000 sq miles (10,000-26,000) sq km, according to the seasons.

Main deserts: Sahara (the largest in the world), about 3,474,927 miles (9,000,000 sq km); Kalahari, about 200,000 sq miles (517,998 sq km).

Largest islands: Madagascar, 226,658 sq miles (587,041 sq km); Socotra, 1,382 sq miles (3,579 sq km); Réunion, 969 sq miles (2,510 sq km).

World's highest sand dunes: Dunes in the Sahara Desert can be up to 3 miles (5 km) long and 1,410 ft (430 m) high.

World's highest temperature: In 1922 the temperature in Al'Azizya (Libya) reached 136.4°F (58°C) in the shade.

World's largest man-made lake: Lake Volta (Ghana), which was formed by the Akosombo Dam, covers an area of 3,275 miles (8,482 sq km).

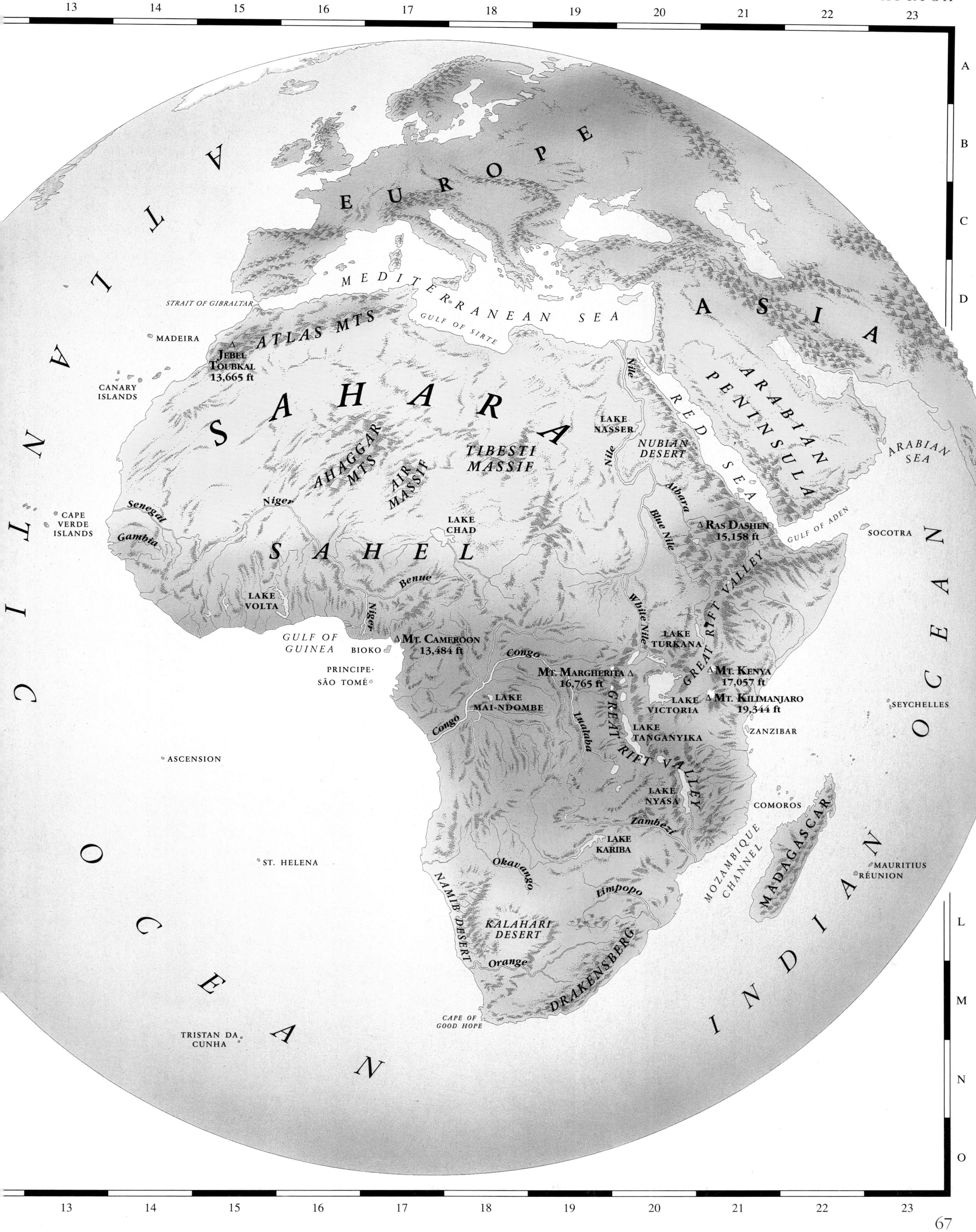

13 14 15 16 17 18 19 20 21 22 23

A
B
C
D

ATLANTIC

EUROPE

MEDITERRANEAN SEA

STRAIT OF GIBRALTAR

GULF OF SIRTE

ASIA

ATLAS MTS

MADEIRA

△ JEBEL
TOUBKAL
13,665 ft

CANARY
ISLANDS

SAHARA

LAKE
NASSER

Nile

NUBIAN
DESERT

ARABIAN
PENINSULA

RED SEA

ARABIAN
SEA

AHAGGAR
MTS

AIR
MASSIF

TIBESTI
MASSIF

CAPE
VERDE
ISLANDS

Senegal

Niger

Gambia

Nile

Atbara

Blue Nile

△ RAS DASHEN
15,158 ft

GULF OF ADEN

SOCOTRA

LAKE
CHAD

SAHEL

Benue

Niger

White Nile

LAKE
TURKANA

GULF OF
GUINEA

LAKE
VOLTA

BIOKO

△ MT. CAMEROON
13,484 ft

Congo

MT. MARGHERITA △
16,765 ft

△ MT. KENYA
17,057 ft

GREAT RIFT VALLEY

PRINCIPE·
SÃO TOMÉ

LAKE
MAI-NDOMBE

Congo

Lualaba

LAKE
VICTORIA

△ MT. KILIMANJARO
19,344 ft

SEYCHELLES

ASCENSION

LAKE
TANGANYIKA

ZANZIBAR

GREAT RIFT VALLEY

LAKE
NYASA

COMOROS

Zambezi

MADAGASCAR

ST. HELENA

LAKE
KARIBA

MOZAMBIQUE
CHANNEL

MAURITIUS
RÉUNION

Okavango

Limpopo

INDIAN

NAMIB DESERT

KALAHARI
DESERT

DRAKENSBERG

Orange

OCEAN

L

M

CAPE OF
GOOD HOPE

OCEAN

N

TRISTAN DA
CUNHA

O

13 14 15 16 17 18 19 20 21 22 23

NORTHERN AFRICA

DOMINATING NORTHERN AFRICA is the huge expanse of the Sahara Desert. The climate is wetter along parts of the north coasts, and here citrus fruits, grapes, and dates are grown. Along the Mediterranean coastline tourism is increasingly important. The largest countries in Northern Africa are Egypt, a farming country, and Libya and Algeria, which have rich supplies of oil and natural gas.

The few people who live in the Sahara Desert are mostly nomads, who move from place to place with their sheep and camels. Along the southern edge of the Sahara is an area of semi-desert called the Sahel, which stretches across the countries of Mauritania, Niger, Chad, and Mali. These are among the world's poorest countries. In recent years the people there have suffered terrible famines.

West Africa, which includes the countries of Nigeria, Ghana, Benin and Ivory Coast, is a fertile region in which such crops as coffee, peanuts, and cocoa are grown.

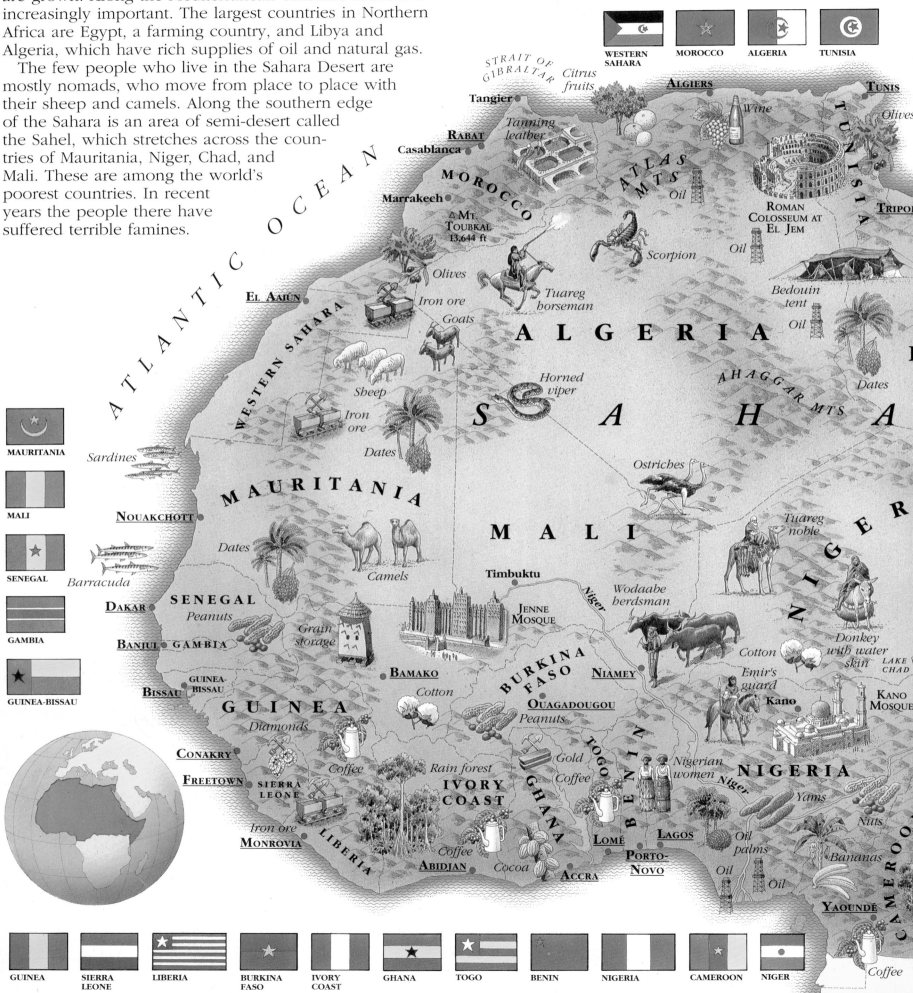

WESTERN SAHARA   MOROCCO   ALGERIA   TUNISIA

MAURITANIA

MALI

SENEGAL

GAMBIA

GUINEA-BISSAU

GUINEA   SIERRA LEONE   LIBERIA   BURKINA FASO   IVORY COAST   GHANA   TOGO   BENIN   NIGERIA   CAMEROON   NIGER

THE PYRAMIDS AND SPHINX

The pyramids of ancient Egypt were built in about 2500 B.C. to contain the mummified bodies of pharaohs, or kings. The three largest are at Giza. The Great Pyramid contains more than two million stone blocks. The Sphinx was probably built to guard the Pharaoh Chephren's body.

Pyramid of Chephren

Great Pyramid of Cheops

Pyramid of Mycerinus

FACTS AND FIGURES

Port Said lies at the entrance to the Suez Canal, which links the Mediterranean and Red Seas.

Longest river: Nile, 4,145 miles (6,670 km).

Highest mountains: Ras Dashen (Ethiopia), 15,158 ft (4,620 m); Mt. Toubkal (Morocco), 13,664 ft (4,165 m).

Largest lake: Lake Chad, area varies from 4,000–10,000 sq miles (10,000–26,000 sq km) according to the season.

ALGERIA Capital: Algiers
BENIN Capital: Porto-Novo
BURKINA FASO Capital: Ouagadougou
CAMEROON Capital: Yaoundé
CENTRAL AFRICAN REPUBLIC Capital: Bangui
CHAD Capital: N'Djamena
DJIBOUTI Capital: Djibouti
EGYPT Capital: Cairo

ETHIOPIA Capital: Addis Ababa
GAMBIA Capital: Banjul
GHANA Capital: Accra
GUINEA Capital: Conakry
GUINEA-BISSAU Capital: Bissau
IVORY COAST Capital: Abidjan
LIBERIA Capital: Monrovia
LIBYA Capital: Tripoli
MALI Capital: Bamako
MAURITANIA Capital: Nouakchott
MOROCCO Capital: Rabat
NIGER Capital: Niamey
NIGERIA Capital: Lagos
SENEGAL Capital: Dakar
SIERRA LEONE Capital: Freetown
SOMALIA Capital: Mogadishu
SUDAN Capital: Khartoum
TOGO Capital: Lomé
TUNISIA Capital: Tunis
WESTERN SAHARA Capital: El Aaiún

SOUTHERN AFRICA

SOUTHERN AFRICA contains a great variety of peoples and landscapes. In the northwest lies the rain forest of the Congo Basin. To the east lie the high grasslands of East Africa, where the peaks of Mt. Kenya and Mt. Kilimanjaro are snow-capped all year long and large herds of wild animals still roam the plains. The countries of Kenya, Uganda, and Tanzania contain rich farmland where coffee, tea, corn, and cotton are grown.

Angola, Zambia, and Zimbabwe are rich in diamonds, iron, and copper. Farther south lies the Kalahari Desert, which covers much of Botswana and Namibia. The world's richest diamond and gold mines are in South Africa. This country is also a major producer of fruit, wheat, cotton, and tobacco.

Until about 100 years ago Europeans called Africa the "Dark Continent," because they knew so little about its interior. Then they began to explore inland and claim areas as colonies. All of these have now been returned to the Africans, except for South Africa. Under a system of apartheid, or racial separation, South Africa's black population is governed by a small number of white people. This has caused considerable unrest and violence. In 1990 the government promised to end apartheid.

THE GREAT RIFT VALLEY

The Great Rift Valley is the largest crack in the earth's crust, stretching 5,400 miles (8,700 km) from Syria in the north, through the Red Sea to Mozambique in southern Africa. It is in East Africa that the scenery of the Rift Valley is most spectacular. In Kenya the walls of the valley rise almost straight up for 4,000 ft (1,250 m).

EQUATORIAL GUINEA

GABON

CONGO

ZAIRE

ANGOLA

ZAMBIA

NAMIBIA

BOTSWANA

SOUTH AFRICA

NIGERIA

ATLANTIC OCEAN

CAMEROON

CENTRAL AFRICAN REPUBLIC

Rain forest

Lowland gorilla

Colobus monkey

Crocodile

EQUATL GUINEA

LIBREVILLE

GABON

Elephant

Pygmy hunters

BRAZZAVILLE

KINSHASA

Matadi

Oil

Oil

Tuna

CONGO

Congo

Ubangi

Mbandaka

Kisangani

ZAIRE

Gray parrot

Hippopotamuses

Kasai

Oil palms

Colobus monkey

Buffalo

CABINDA

Hornbill

LUANDA

Coffee

Diamonds

Diamonds

Mackerel

ANGOLA

Benguela

Millet

Cassava

Copper

Zambezi

Z

Ovambo houses

Cattle

VICTORIA FALLS

Lions

Zebra

Anchovies

Gecko

Springbox

NAMIBIA

WINDHOEK

BOTSWANA

GABORONE

KALAHARI DESERT

Pilchards

Bushmen

Oryx

Diamonds

Quiver tree

Orange

Diamonds

Hake

Kimberley

Sheep

SOUTH AF

TABLE MOUNTAIN 3,566 ft

CAPE OF GOOD HOPE

Cape Town

Wine

Ostriches

Port Elizabeth

13   14   15   16   17   18   19   20   21   22   23

SUDAN

ETHIOPIA

SOMALIA

Elephant

UGANDA

Coffee

Cotton

KENYA

Cheetah

Giant groundsel

KAMPALA

MT. KENYA 17,057 ft

Lions

LAKE TURKANA

LAKE VICTORIA

Coffee

NAIROBI

Coconut palms

KIGALI

Wildebeest

Dhow

BUJUMBURA
BURUNDI

Mombasa

Gorilla

Masai herdsman

Dodoma

MT. KILIMANJARO 19,344 ft

Tourism

ZANZIBAR

Chimpanzee

DAR-ES-SALAAM

TANZANIA

Tea

Elephants

ALDABRA ISLANDS

Leopard

COMOROS

Copper

Rhinoceros

COMOROS

Mangoes

Ndola

MAYOTTE (Fr)

Copper

Crested hornbill

MALAWI

Vanilla pods

LILONGWE

KARIBA DAM

Plowshare tortoise

LUSAKA

Blantyre

Lemur

Long-tailed ground roller

LAKE KARIBA

Bananas

Tea

ANTANANARIVO

ZIMBABWE

HARARE

ZIMBABWE

Baobab tree

MADAGASCAR

Soapstone carving

Black lemur

Bulawayo

Chameleon

GREAT ZIMBABWE

Beira

Limpopo

MOZAMBIQUE CHANNEL

MOZAMBIQUE

Octopus tree

Gold

Cashew nuts

Giraffes

Coelacanth

PRETORIA

Johannesburg

MAPUTO

Shrimps

MBABANE

Zulu

SWAZILAND

SWAZILAND

MASERU
LESOTHO

Citrus fruits

LESOTHO

Durban

Tourism

Umtata

Pineapples   *Lobster*

INDIAN OCEAN

0   200   400   600   800 Kilometers

0   100   200   300   400   500 Miles

FACTS AND FIGURES

Zebra in the plains of Kenya. In recent years their numbers have been greatly reduced by hunting.

Highest mountains:
Mt. Kilimanjaro (Kenya), 19,344 ft (5,896 m); Mt. Kenya (Kenya), 17,057 ft (5,199 m).

Longest rivers:
Congo, 2,900 miles (4,667 km); Zambezi, 1,700 miles (2,756 km).

Largest lakes: Lake Victoria, 26,800 sq miles (69,400 sq km); Lake Tanganyika, 13,860 sq miles (32,900 sq km).

Deepest lake: Lake Tanganyika, 4,708 ft (1,435 m).

Largest cities: Kinshasa (Zaire), 3,000,000; Cape Town (South Africa), 1,790,000.

ANGOLA
Capital: Luanda

BOTSWANA
Capital: Gaborone

BURUNDI
Capital: Bujumbura

COMOROS
Capital: Moroni

CONGO
Capital: Brazzaville

EQUATORIAL GUINEA
Capital: Malabo

GABON
Capital: Libreville

KENYA
Capital: Nairobi

LESOTHO
Capital: Maseru

MADAGASCAR
Capital: Antananarivo

MALAWI
Capital: Lilongwe

MOZAMBIQUE
Capital: Maputo

NAMIBIA
Capital: Windhoek

RWANDA
Capital: Kigali

SOUTH AFRICA
National capital: Pretoria
Seat of government: Cape Town

SWAZILAND
Capital: Mbabane

TANZANIA
Capital: Dar-es-Salaam

UGANDA
Capital: Kampala

ZAIRE
Capital: Kinshasa

ZAMBIA
Capital: Lusaka

ZIMBABWE
Capital: Harare

OCEANIA

OCEANIA IS THE SMALLEST of the continents and it has fewer people than any other continent except Antarctica. Oceania is sometimes called Australasia, after Australia, which is the only large piece of land it contains. The continent also includes the islands of New Guinea and New Zealand, and thousands of tiny islands scattered across the Pacific Ocean, many of which are too small to show on the map.

Australia, New Zealand and New Guinea were once joined to the other southern continents, but over millions of years they split off and drifted into the Pacific Ocean. Because Oceania is so isolated, many of the plants and animals which have evolved there are not found anywhere else in the world. The pouched mammals of Australia, such as the kangaroo, wallaby, and koala, and the flightless birds of New Zealand, such as the kiwi and the kakapo, are examples of this.

One of the Fijian islands.

The Pacific islands have been formed in a number of ways. Some of them are the tips of mountains or volcanoes which rise up from the ocean bed. Others are formed of coral, made up of the skeletons of millions of tiny sea creatures.

The Pacific islands fall into three groups, depending on their position in the ocean. In the middle of the Pacific are the Polynesian Islands, the biggest of which are the Hawaiian Islands. By the Stone Age, the light-skinned Polynesian people had become great explorers and navigators. They sailed all over the Pacific in their small double canoes, finding their way from the position of the stars and the patterns of the waves. The Maori people of New Zealand are descended from Polynesians who settled there in about A.D. 900.

The city of Perth, Australia.

The Micronesian Islands are situated in the western Pacific. Like the Polynesians, the Micronesians were great seafarers, and traded throughout the region. The dark-skinned Melanesian people live on the islands closest to Australia and are related to the Australian Aborigines. Today, tourism is an important industry in the Pacific islands, and this has brought many changes to the islanders' way of life.

Europeans first began to settle in Oceania in the 18th century. Most of the people who now live in Australia and New Zealand are descendants of settlers from the United Kingdom. More recently, immigrants have also come from other parts of Europe, Polynesia, and the Far East.

Maori carving, New Zealand.

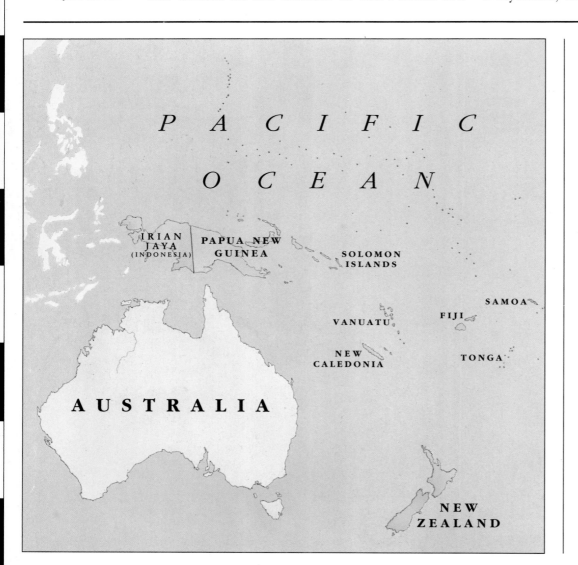

PACIFIC OCEAN

IRIAN JAYA (INDONESIA)

PAPUA NEW GUINEA

SOLOMON ISLANDS

VANUATU

FIJI

SAMOA

NEW CALEDONIA

TONGA

AUSTRALIA

NEW ZEALAND

FACTS ABOUT OCEANIA

Area: 3,445,197 sq miles (8,923,000 sq km). Oceania is the smallest of the continents and covers only six percent of the world's land area.

Population: 25,800,000. Fewer people live in Oceania than any other continent, except Antarctica.

Number of independent countries: 11.

Largest country: Australia, 2,967,928 sq miles (7,686,884 sq km).

Most populated country: Australia, 16,506,000.

Largest cities: Sydney (Australia), 3,364,858; Melbourne (Australia), 2,832,893; Brisbane (Australia), 1,149,400; Perth (Australia), 994,472; Adelaide (Australia), 977,721; Auckland (New Zealand), 850,000.

Highest mountains: Mt. Wilhelm (Papua New Guinea), 14,793 ft (4,509 m); Mt. Cook (New Zealand), 12,349 ft (3,764 m); Mt. Kosciusko (Australia), 7,310 ft (2,228 m).

Longest river: Murray-Darling (Australia), 2,330 miles (3,750 km).

Largest deserts: Gibson Desert, Great Sandy Desert, Great Victoria Desert, Simpson Desert (all in Australia).

Largest islands: New Guinea, 312,168 sq miles (808,510 sq km); South Island, New Zealand, 58,093 sq miles (150,460 sq km).

Largest lakes: Lake Eyre (Australia), 3,436 sq miles (8,900 sq km); Lake Gairdner (Australia), 3,000 sq miles (7,770 sq km); Lake Torrens (Australia), 2,231 sq miles (5,780 sq km).

Oldest rocks: The oldest rocks ever found on Earth are zircon crystals from the Jack Hills near Perth, Australia. They are 4.3 billion years old.

I N D I A N

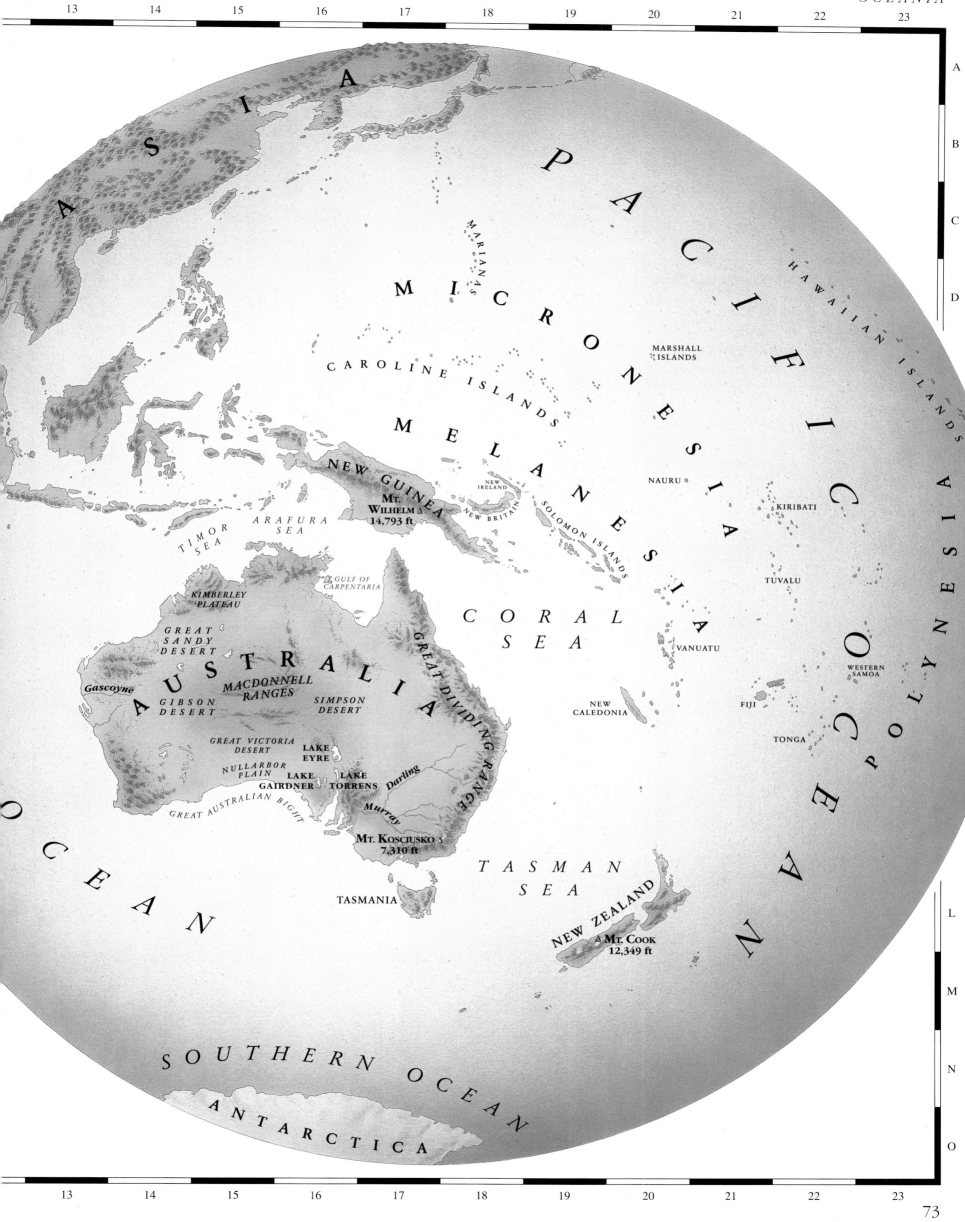

ASIA

PACIFIC

MICRONESIA

MELANESIA

POLYNESIA

PACIFIC OCEAN

HAWAIIAN ISLANDS

MARIANAS

CAROLINE ISLANDS

MARSHALL ISLANDS

NEW GUINEA
MT. WILHELM △ 14,793 ft

NEW IRELAND

NEW BRITAIN

SOLOMON ISLANDS

NAURU

KIRIBATI

TUVALU

TIMOR SEA

ARAFURA SEA

GULF OF CARPENTARIA

CORAL SEA

VANUATU

WESTERN SAMOA

KIMBERLEY PLATEAU

GREAT SANDY DESERT

AUSTRALIA

MACDONNELL RANGES

GREAT DIVIDING RANGE

NEW CALEDONIA

FIJI

TONGA

Gascoyne

GIBSON DESERT

SIMPSON DESERT

GREAT VICTORIA DESERT

LAKE EYRE

NULLARBOR PLAIN

LAKE GAIRDNER

LAKE TORRENS

Darling

Murray

GREAT AUSTRALIAN BIGHT

MT. KOSCIUSKO △ 7,310 ft

TASMAN SEA

TASMANIA

NEW ZEALAND
△ MT. COOK 12,349 ft

INDIAN OCEAN

SOUTHERN OCEAN

ANTARCTICA

AUSTRALIA

AUSTRALIA is a country and a continent. It is almost as big as the United States. Much of the country is hot and dry, especially in the middle where there are deserts. Few people live in these dry areas, but there are large sheep and cattle farms called "stations" and some mining. East of the hills and mountains of the Great Dividing Range and on the island of Tasmania the climate is wetter, and it is here that most people live. Two-thirds of all Australians live in the small number of large cities, particularly the state capitals, such as Sydney, Melbourne, and Brisbane. The population of Australia is only 16 million people, compared with 245 million in the United States.

Millions of years ago, Australia drifted away from the other continents of the world. As a result, many of the plants and animals which have evolved there are not found anywhere else in the world. Many of the mammals, such as kangaroos and wombats, are marsupials that rear their young in pouches on their stomachs.

The first inhabitants of Australia were the Aborigines, who arrived about 40,000 years ago. Europeans did not settle in Australia until 200 years ago. Since 1945 the population has doubled, with people coming to Australia from many parts of the world.

THE GREAT BARRIER REEF

The Great Barrier Reef is a maze of about 2,500 coral reefs and islands stretching 1,200 miles (2,000 km) along the coast of Queensland. It contains over 300 species of coral and thousands of fish. Coral is formed by millions of tiny sea animals called polyps, which cement themselves together. The Great Barrier Reef is slowly being eaten away by creatures called crown-of-thorns starfishes. In order to protect the reef from further destruction by both humans and natural causes, the Great Barrier Reef Marine Park has been formed.

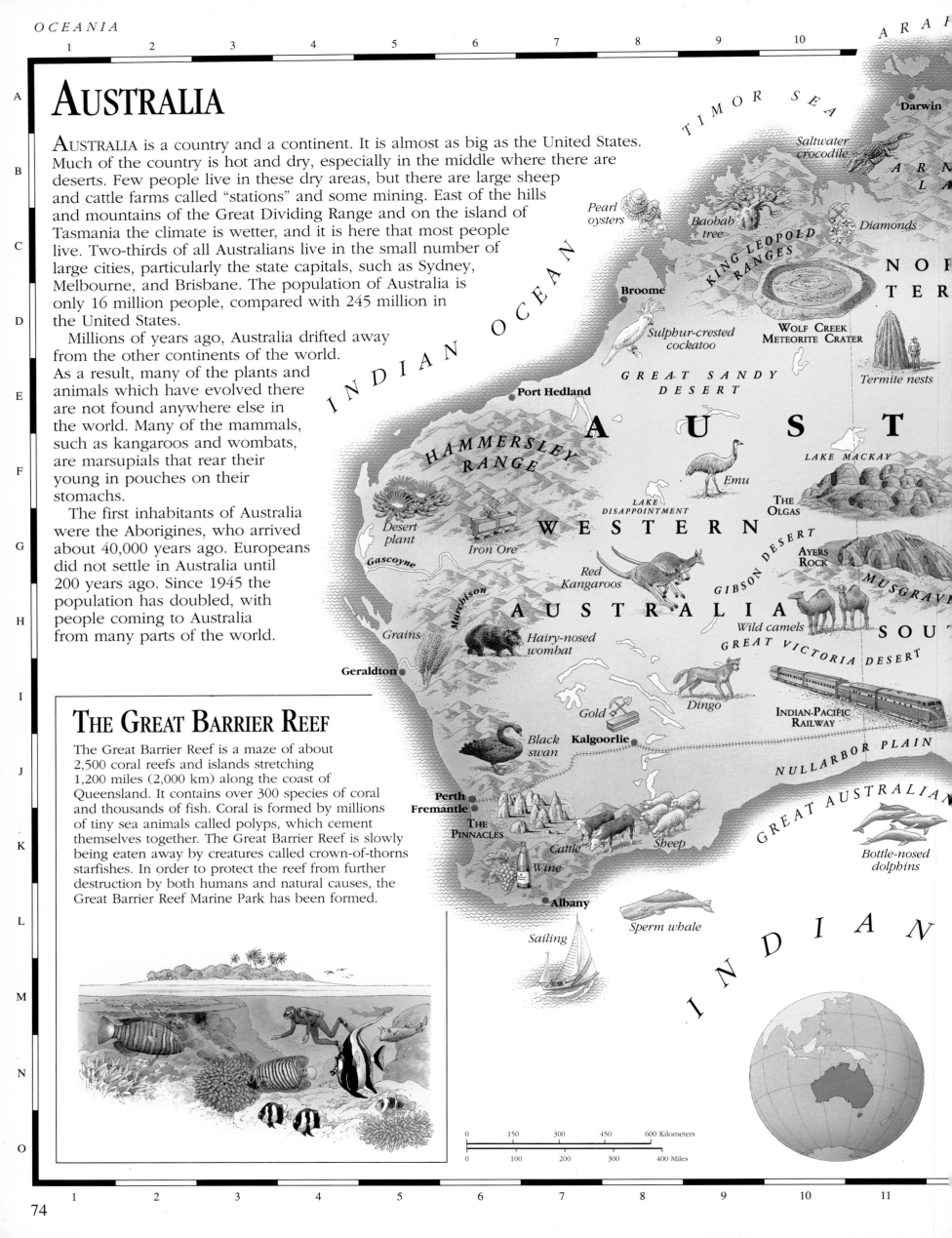

Darwin · Saltwater crocodile · Pearl oysters · Baobab tree · Diamonds · KING LEOPOLD RANGES · NORTHERN TERR · Broome · Sulphur-crested cockatoo · WOLF CREEK METEORITE CRATER · Termite nests · INDIAN OCEAN · Port Hedland · GREAT SANDY DESERT · AUST · HAMMERSLEY RANGE · Emu · LAKE MACKAY · THE OLGAS · LAKE DISAPPOINTMENT · WESTERN · Desert plant · Iron Ore · Gascoyne · GIBSON DESERT · AYERS ROCK · MUSGRAVE · Red Kangaroos · AUSTRALIA · SOUTH · Murchison · Grains · Hairy-nosed wombat · Wild camels · GREAT VICTORIA DESERT · Geraldton · Gold · Dingo · INDIAN-PACIFIC RAILWAY · Black swan · Kalgoorlie · NULLARBOR PLAIN · Perth · Fremantle · THE PINNACLES · GREAT AUSTRALIAN · Cattle · Sheep · Bottle-nosed dolphins · Wine · Albany · Sperm whale · Sailing · INDIAN · TIMOR SEA · ARAF

0 150 300 450 600 Kilometers
0 100 200 300 400 Miles

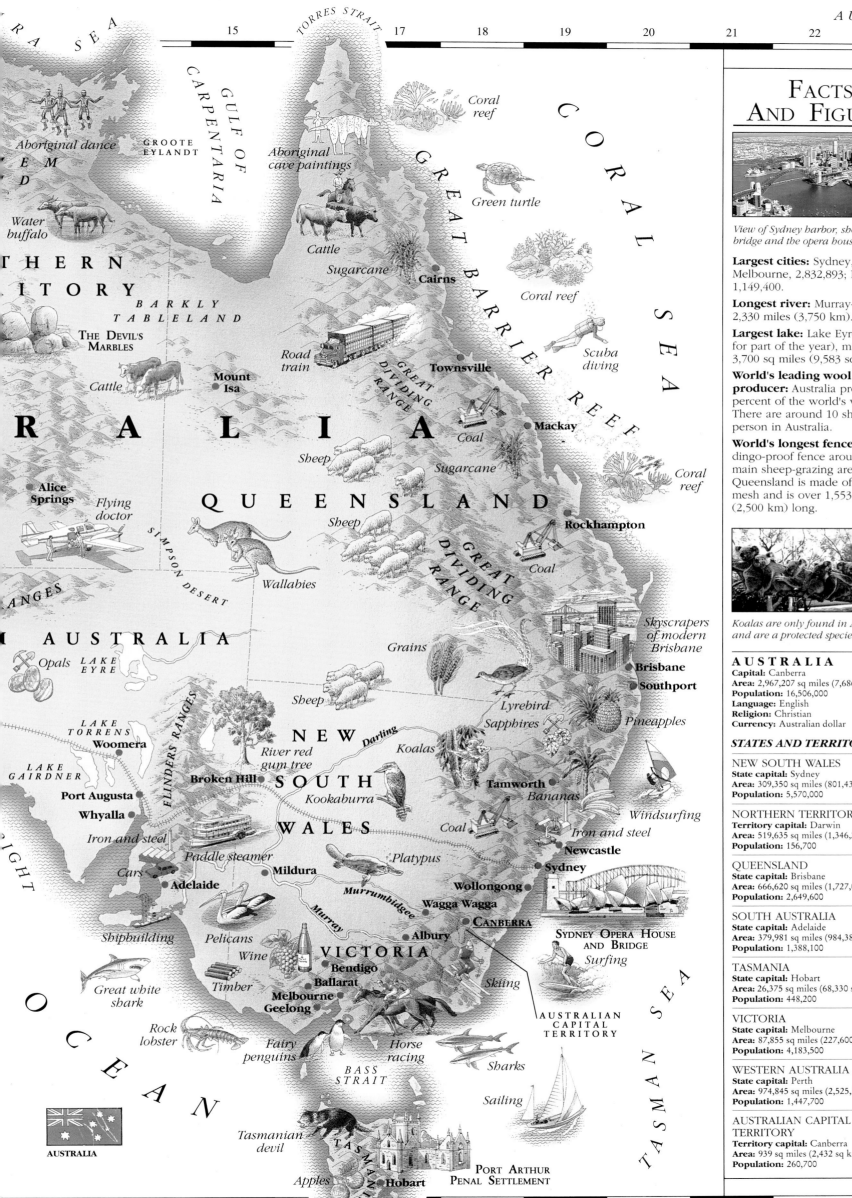

TORRES STRAIT

15   17   18   19   20   21   22   23

Aboriginal dance

GULF OF CARPENTARIA

GROOTE EYLANDT

Water buffalo

Aboriginal cave paintings

Cattle

Coral reef

Green turtle

GREAT BARRIER REEF

CORAL SEA

Sugarcane

Cairns

Coral reef

Scuba diving

...THERN ...TORY

BARKLY TABLELAND

THE DEVIL'S MARBLES

Road train

GREAT DIVIDING RANGE

Townsville

Cattle

Mount Isa

Coal

Mackay

Coral reef

...RALIA

Sheep

Sugarcane

Alice Springs

Flying doctor

QUEENSLAND

Sheep

Rockhampton

SIMPSON DESERT

Wallabies

GREAT DIVIDING RANGE

Coal

...AUSTRALIA

Grains

Skyscrapers of modern Brisbane

Opals

LAKE EYRE

Sheep

Brisbane

Southport

Lyrebird

Sapphires

Pineapples

LAKE TORRENS

FLINDERS RANGES

River red gum tree

NEW SOUTH WALES

Darling

Koalas

Woomera

Broken Hill

Kookaburra

Tamworth

Bananas

LAKE GAIRDNER

Coal

Iron and steel

Port Augusta

Whyalla

Iron and steel

Paddle steamer

Platypus

Newcastle

Windsurfing

Sydney

Cars

Mildura

Murrumbidgee

Wollongong

Adelaide

Pelicans

Murray

Wagga Wagga

CANBERRA

Shipbuilding

Wine

VICTORIA

Albury

SYDNEY OPERA HOUSE AND BRIDGE

Great white shark

Timber

Bendigo

Ballarat

Surfing

Skiing

Rock lobster

Melbourne

Geelong

Fairy penguins

Horse racing

Sharks

OCEAN

BASS STRAIT

Sailing

AUSTRALIA

Tasmanian devil

TASMANIA

Apples

Hobart

PORT ARTHUR PENAL SETTLEMENT

TASMAN SEA

13   14   15   18   19   20   21   22   23

A
B
C
D
E
F
G
H
I
J
K
L
M
N
O

FACTS AND FIGURES

View of Sydney harbor, showing the bridge and the opera house.

Largest cities: Sydney, 3,364,858; Melbourne, 2,832,893; Brisbane, 1,149,400.

Longest river: Murray-Darling, 2,330 miles (3,750 km).

Largest lake: Lake Eyre (dry for part of the year), max. of 3,700 sq miles (9,583 sq km).

World's leading wool producer: Australia produces 25 percent of the world's wool. There are around 10 sheep per person in Australia.

World's longest fence: The dingo-proof fence around the main sheep-grazing areas in Queensland is made of wire mesh and is over 1,553 miles (2,500 km) long.

Koalas are only found in Australia and are a protected species.

AUSTRALIA
Capital: Canberra
Area: 2,967,207 sq miles (7,686,848 sq km)
Population: 16,506,000
Language: English
Religion: Christian
Currency: Australian dollar

STATES AND TERRITORIES:

NEW SOUTH WALES
State capital: Sydney
Area: 309,350 sq miles (801,430 sq km)
Population: 5,570,000

NORTHERN TERRITORY
Territory capital: Darwin
Area: 519,635 sq miles (1,346,200 sq km)
Population: 156,700

QUEENSLAND
State capital: Brisbane
Area: 666,620 sq miles (1,727,000 sq km)
Population: 2,649,600

SOUTH AUSTRALIA
State capital: Adelaide
Area: 379,981 sq miles (984,380 sq km)
Population: 1,388,100

TASMANIA
State capital: Hobart
Area: 26,375 sq miles (68,330 sq km)
Population: 448,200

VICTORIA
State capital: Melbourne
Area: 87,855 sq miles (227,600 sq km)
Population: 4,183,500

WESTERN AUSTRALIA
State capital: Perth
Area: 974,845 sq miles (2,525,500 sq km)
Population: 1,447,700

AUSTRALIAN CAPITAL TERRITORY
Territory capital: Canberra
Area: 939 sq miles (2,432 sq km)
Population: 260,700

NEW ZEALAND

NEW ZEALAND lies in the Pacific Ocean, about 1,000 miles (1,600 km) southeast of Australia. The country is made up of two main islands: the North Island and the South Island. Most people live on the North Island, which has a warm, tropical climate.

The first people to reach New Zealand were the Maoris, who started to settle there around A.D. 900. They sailed to New Zealand from the Polynesian Islands in small, open boats. The first European to sight the country was the Dutch explorer, Abel Tasman, in 1642. New Zealand became a British colony in 1840 and an independent country in 1907.

Today the population is a mixture of Maoris and people of British descent. The country's wealth comes from industry and farming, particularly raising cattle and sheep. New Zealand is the world's biggest exporter of lamb and second largest exporter of dairy products.

HOT SPRINGS

In the region around Rotorua, on the North Island, hot water bubbles out of the ground. In some places there is such pressure underground that water is forced out in a jet called a geyser, reaching heights of up to 230 ft (70 m). The steam produced in this area is used to drive electric power stations.

Map labels

Oysters
Tourism
Kauri pine
Snapper
Whangarei
Sailing
HAURAKI GULF
Auckland
Iron and steel
Windsurfing
Dairy cattle
BAY OF PLENTY
Hamilton
Tauranga
Maori carving
NORTH ISLAND
Kiwi fruit
Rotorua
Waikato
MT. TARANAKI (MT. EGMONT) 8,261 ft
LAKE TAUPO
Gisborne
Oil and gas
New Plymouth
Haka (Maori dance)
HAWKE BAY
Napier
Gannets
Wanganui
Hastings
Snapper
Palmerston North
TASMAN BAY
COOK STRAIT
Nelson
Blenheim
WELLINGTON
PARLIAMENT BUILDINGS (WELLINGTON)
NEW ZEALAND
Apples
NEW ZEALAND
Greymouth
Kiwi
Sheep
Kaikoura
MT. COOK 12,349 ft
TASMAN SEA
SOUTH ISLAND
SOUTHERN ALPS
CANTERBURY PLAINS
Sperm whale
CHRISTCHURCH CATHEDRAL
Christchurch
PACIFIC OCEAN
Takahe
Textiles
Timaru
MILFORD SOUND
Skiing
Sheep
Tarakihi
Kakapo
Royal albatross
Apricots
Dunedin
Rugby
FOVEAUX STRAIT
Invercargill
Rock lobster
STEWART ISLAND

FACTS AND FIGURES

The city of Auckland lies between Waitemata and Manukau Harbors and is a center for water sports.

NEW ZEALAND
Capital: Wellington
Area: 103,736 sq miles (268,676 sq km)
Population: 3,339,000
Languages: English, Maori
Religion: Christian
Currency: New Zealand dollar
Government: Monarchy

Largest lake: Lake Taupo, 234 sq miles (606 sq km).

Longest river: Waikato, 264 miles (425 km).

Largest cities: Auckland, 850,000; Wellington, 350,000; Christchurch, 320,000.

Long inlets of sea cut into the land on the western coast of the South Island. The area is called Fiordland, after the Norwegian fjords.

Scale
0 50 100 150 200 250 Kilometers
0 50 100 150 Miles

INDEX

This index contains the names of places shown on continental and country maps. The page number is given in bold type after the place name. The grid reference follows in lighter type (see also page 13, How to Use This Atlas).

ACKNOWLEDGMENTS

Dorling Kindersley would like to thank the following:
Kate Woodward and Anna Kunst for research, Chris Scollen and Richard Czapnik for additional design help, and Struan Reid for editorial assistance.

Picture Research Cynthia Hole

Political Maps Luciano Corbella

Picture credits
(r = right, l = left, t = top, c = centre, b = bottom)

Australian Overseas Information Service, London 75tr, 75br
Australian Tourist Commission, London 72tr

de Beers 66rl
Charles Bowman 16br, 25tr, 34c, 51tr, 51tl, 52tl, 59tr, 59br, 76tl,
Canadian High Commission 16tc, 19tc
Caribbean Tourist Office 27tr
The J. Allan Cash Photolibrary 6tr, 6bl, 12tl, 12br, 20tr, 23br, 23bl, 36tl, 36br, 45tl, 76br,
Lester Cheeseman 52bc, 65tl, 65tr, 65bc, 66tr
Chilean Embassy 33br, 33bl
Chinese Tourist Office 63br
Bruce Coleman Ltd / Fritz Prenzel 7cl, Commission of the European Communities 34tl
Susan Cunningham 31br
Richard Czapnik 66c
Egyptian Tourist Office 57tr, 69tr

Chris Fairclough Colour Library 12c, 21tr, 43tr, 43br, 45c, 52tr, 72c, 72bl,
Fiat Press Office 46cr
French Railways Ltd 39cr
Susan Griggs Agency / Rob Cousins 7tl; George Hall 12tr
Robert Harding Picture Library 6tl
Hutchison Library / John Dowman 6br; Anwa Tully 12bl
The Image Bank / Guido Rossi 12bc
Italian State Tourist Office 46tl
Kenyan Tourist Office 71tr
Anna Kunst 55tr, 55cr
Keith Lye 16cl, 28tl, 28bc, 52tr, 57br, 63tr
Norwegian Tourist Office 14tr, 15tr

Peruvian Embassy 28tr, 31tr
Roger Priddy 34tr, 36tr, 39tr, 39br, 46cl
South American Pictures 33tl
Spanish National Tourist Office 49tr
The Telegraph Colour Library 41bl
Travel Photo International 7tr, 7cr, 41tr, 41br, 43cr, 45br, 49br
Zefa Picture Library 12cr
Zentrale Farbbild Agentur / D. Frobisch 7br

Every effort has been made to trace the copyright holders and we apologise in advance for any unintentional omissions. We would be pleased to insert the appropriate acknowledgment in any subsequent edition of this book.